Hallucinogens

Hallucinogens

Other books in the History of Drugs series:

THE HISTORY OF DRUGS

Hallucinogens

EDITED BY MARY E. WILLIAMS

Bruce Glassman, *Vice President*
Bonnie Szumski, *Publisher*
Helen Cothran, *Managing Editor*

GREENHAVEN PRESS
An imprint of Thomson Gale, a part of The Thomson Corporation

THOMSON
™
GALE

Detroit • New York • San Francisco • San Diego • New Haven, Conn.
Waterville, Maine • London • Munich

S

© 2005 Thomson Gale, a part of The Thomson Corporation.

Thomson and Star Logo are trademarks and Gale and Greenhaven Press are registered trademarks used herein under license.

For more information, contact
Greenhaven Press
27500 Drake Rd.
Farmington Hills, MI 48331-3535
Or you can visit our Internet site at http://www.gale.com

Cover credit: © Ted Streshinsky/CORBIS
Library of Congress, 103

LIBRARY OF CONGRESS CATALOGING-IN-PUBLICATION DATA

Hallucinogens / Mary E. Williams, book editor.
   p. cm. — (The history of drugs)
Includes bibliographical references and index.
ISBN 0-7377-1959-1 (lib. : alk. paper)
   1. Hallucinogenic drugs—History. 2. Hallucinogenic plants—History. I. Williams, Mary E., 1960– . II. Series.
RM324.8.H344 2005
615'.7883—dc22

                                          2004052394

Printed in the United States of America

CONTENTS

Chapter Three: Hallucinogens and the Counterculture

CHAPTER FOUR: CONTEMPORARY VIEWS ON HALLUCINOGENS

patients cope with pain and reduce their anxiety
as death approaches.

FOREWORD

Drugs are chemical compounds that affect the functioning of the body and the mind. While the U.S. Food, Drug, and Cosmetic Act defines drugs as substances intended for use in the cure, mitigation, treatment, or prevention of disease, humans have long used drugs for recreational and religious purposes as well as for healing and medicinal purposes. Depending on context, then, the term *drug* provokes various reactions. In recent years, the widespread problem of substance abuse and addiction has often given the word *drug* a negative connotation. Nevertheless, drugs have made possible a revolution in the way modern doctors treat disease. The tension arising from the myriad ways drugs can be used is what makes their history so fascinating. Positioned at the intersection of science, anthropology, religion, therapy, sociology, and cultural studies, the history of drugs offers intriguing insights on medical discovery, cultural conflict, and the bright and dark sides of human innovation and experimentation.

Drugs are commonly grouped in three broad categories: over-the-counter drugs, prescription drugs, and illegal drugs. A historical examination of drugs, however, invites students and interested readers to observe the development of these categories and to see how arbitrary and changeable they can be. A particular drug's status is often the result of social and political forces that may not necessarily reflect its medicinal effects or its potential dangers. Marijuana, for example, is currently classified as an illegal Schedule I substance by the U.S. federal government, defining it as a drug with a high potential for abuse and no currently accepted medical use. Yet in 1850 it was included in the U.S. *Pharmacopoeia* as a medicine, and solutions and tinctures containing cannabis were frequently prescribed for relieving pain and inducing sleep. In the 1930s, after smokable marijuana had gained notoriety as a recreational intoxicant, the Federal Bureau of Narcotics launched a misinformation campaign against the drug, claiming that it commonly induced insanity and murderous violence. While today's medical experts no longer make such claims about marijuana, they continue to disagree about the drug's long-term effects and medicinal potential. Most interestingly, several states have passed medical marijuana initiatives, which allow seriously ill patients compassionate access to the drug under state law—although these patients can still be prosecuted for marijuana use under federal law. Marijuana's illegal status, then, is not as fixed or final as the federal government's current schedule might suggest. Examining marijuana from a historical perspective offers readers the chance to develop a more sophisticated and critically informed view of a controversial and politically charged subject. It also encourages students to learn about aspects of medicine, history, and culture that may receive scant attention in textbooks.

Each book in Greenhaven's The History of Drugs series chronicles a particular substance or group of related drugs— discussing the appearance and earliest use of the drug in initial chapters and more recent and contemporary controversies in later chapters. With the incorporation of both primary and secondary sources written by physicians, anthropologists, psychologists, historians, social analysts, and lawmakers, each anthology provides an engaging panoramic view of its subject. Selections include a variety of readings, including book excerpts, government documents, newspaper editorials, academic articles, and personal narratives. The editors of each volume aim to include accounts of notable incidents, ideas, subcultures, or individuals connected with the drug's history as well as perspectives on the effects, benefits, dangers, and legal status of the drug.

Every volume in the series includes an introductory essay that presents a broad overview of the drug in question. The annotated table of contents and comprehensive index help readers quickly locate material of interest. Each selection is prefaced by a summary of the article that also provides any necessary historical context and biographical information on the author. Several other research aids are also present, including excerpts of supplementary material, a time line of relevant historical events, the U.S. government's current drug schedule, a fact sheet detailing drug effects, and a bibliography of helpful sources.

Greenhaven Press's The History of Drugs series gives readers a unique and informative introduction to an often-ignored facet of scientific and cultural history. The contents of each anthology provide a valuable resource for general readers as well as for students interested in medicine, political science, philosophy, and social studies.

INTRODUCTION

Hallucinogen is the term most commonly used to define a group of drugs that induce distorted or bizarre sensory perceptions, an altered sense of time and space, strange thoughts, and changes in mood and identity awareness. Hallucinogens, however, do not generally produce full-blown hallucinations, which are unreal images or illusions that are perceived as real. Hence, certain investigators prefer the term *psychedelic*, which emphasizes the consciousness-changing properties of drugs such as LSD, psilocybin, peyote, and mescaline.

Mind-altering substances have a long and complex history. Since early times, humans have ingested psychoactive plants, often as part of communal religious rituals or during rites-of-passage involving visions and excursions to the world of spirits and sacred beings. Healers, shamans, and spiritual leaders would use hallucinogens to commune with deities or to identify and cure various illnesses. Many ancient religious and historical texts, moreover, contain references to hallucinogens. The Hindu *Rig-Veda*, for example, contains dozens of references and prayers to soma, a drink made from a psychoactive fungus, which was said to grant immortality and divine inspiration. Ancient Greeks participating in the Eleusinian Mysteries—a symbolic journey to retrieve the goddess Persephone from the underworld—drank a beverage believed to contain ergot, a hallucinogenic mold. In the 1600s, Spanish colonialists passed laws banning peyote, a hallucinogenic cactus that had been used ceremonially for centuries by native peoples of the Americas.

Peyote turned out to be the first hallucinogenic drug that attracted the interest of Western scientists in the nineteenth century. In the 1880s German pharmacologist Louis Lewin published his book *Phantastica*, which contained a description of peyote intoxication and notes on the effects of the drug on animals. In 1897 controversial British physician Havelock Ellis wrote an article for a medical journal describing his own personal experience taking peyote, claiming it to be an "orgy of vision" abounding with images of iridescent flowers and insects. Both Lewin and Ellis concluded that such "vision-inducing" drugs merited further scientific investigation, but it was not until the twentieth century that researchers began more serious examinations of the properties of hallucinogens.

In 1938 Swiss chemist Albert Hofmann first synthesized LSD-25 (lysergic acid diethylamide), a derivative of rye ergot, during an investigation of potential circulatory stimulants. Although researchers noted that the drug caused restlessness in animals, further testing was abandoned because pharmacologists showed little interest in it. Five years later, however, Hofmann produced another batch of LSD-25, thinking that the researchers in his lab might discover other uses for the drug. During the synthesizing process, Hofmann accidentally absorbed a small amount of LSD through his fingertips and subsequently experienced a dreamlike intoxicated state. He then decided to conduct an intentional test with a larger amount of the drug—with himself as the subject—and discovered the alternately horrifying and euphoric effects that LSD could induce. He concluded that "LSD . . . would have to be of use in pharmacology, in neurology, and especially in psychiatry, and . . . would attract the interest of concerned specialists."

LSD and other hallucinogens such as psilocybin and mescaline did attract considerable attention among psychiatric researchers in the 1950s. Initially, scientists believed that experiments with these drugs would lead to a better understanding of psychosis, but researchers became even more enthusiastic about the therapeutic potential of hallucinogens. In the early 1950s several researchers recommended LSD as an aid in psychoanalysis, as it seemed to act as a "super accelerant" for talk therapy, deepening and intensifying the therapeutic process—and shortening the time necessary for the treatment of various disorders. In addition, studies revealed that hallucinogen-assisted treatment could work for people who had generally been seen as poor candidates for therapy: alcoholics, narcotics addicts, sociopaths, autistic children, concentration-camp survivors, people with personality disorders, and the terminally ill. Bill Wilson, the cofounder of Alcoholics Anonymous, had been sober for twenty years when he volunteered to take LSD in 1956. Wilson stated that the drug held great promise for alcoholics and drug addicts, as it seemed to dramatically "deflate the ego" and precipitate a profound spiritual transformation, "making the influx of God's grace possible." By the early 1960s, several U.S. institutions—including some major universities, the National Institute of Mental Health, and the Central Intelligence Agency—had conducted experiments with hallucinogens on thousands of people.

It was in the 1960s, however, that conflicts developed between those who supported the research and development of therapeutic hallucinogens and those who wanted to protect the public from the dangers of these potent drugs. One researcher who played a prominent role at this time was Timothy Leary, a clinical psychologist who taught at Harvard University. Through the university's Center for Research in Personality, Leary and his colleague, Richard Alpert, conducted studies involving psilocybin and LSD. One early experiment examined the effect of psilocybin on recidivist convicts. Leary and Alpert took the drug along with the prisoners in a comfortable, relaxing environment and then discussed the experiences at length with the prisoners. In addition, the researchers helped arrange employment and housing for them after their release dates. A year's follow-up survey revealed that none of the released subjects had had to return to prison, suggesting that the psilocybin had transformed the prisoners. However, as many Harvard faculty members pointed out, Leary had not used a control group to eliminate significant variables, and his participation in the experiment had undermined his objectivity.

Leary and Alpert continued to conduct informal and unconventional experiments with hallucinogens, sparking rumors that local undergraduates were being given psilocybin and LSD. Accordingly, Leary and Alpert signed an agreement with Harvard University not to administer drugs to undergraduates. In addition, the Massachusetts State Department of Health warned the researchers that in order for their experiments to be legal a physician had to be present. However, authorities became further alarmed in the fall of 1962, with reports of the spread of black-market LSD in the Harvard area. While there were no laws then against the possession or use of hallucinogens, such drugs were presumed to be available only through therapists, clinicians, or researchers. Concerned experts, such as Dana Farnsworth of the Harvard Medical Service, began issuing warnings about the unauthorized and nonscientific uses of hallucinogens: "The ingestion of [LSD] can precipitate psychotic reactions in some apparently normal persons. It has been known to increase slight depressions into suicidal ones and to produce schizophrenia-like reactions."

Harvard was not the only place where hallucinogens had apparently escaped from the laboratory. In July 1962, researchers Sidney Cohen and Keith Ditman drew attention to the phenomenon of the California "LSD party" in an article published in the *Journal of the American Medical Association*. The growing misuse of hallucinogens could be traced to irresponsible and unstable therapists who derived an "intoxicating sense of power" by giving these drugs to others, they wrote. More and more youths—college kids as well as "maladjusted rebels"—were taking LSD, increasing the chances for dangerous reactions, Cohen explained. Disquieted by projects like Leary's, Cohen concluded that LSD must be "restricted to investigators in institutions and hospitals where the patients' protection is greater and appropriate countermeasures are available in case of adverse reactions."

Motivated by the concerns of experts such as Cohen, Congress passed a law in 1963 that gave the Food and Drug Administration (FDA) control over all new investigational drugs. Subsequently, therapists and hallucinogen researchers had to obtain government permission to conduct their experiments. Many researchers were required to hand over their remaining supplies of hallucinogens.

In the meantime, both Leary and Alpert were fired from Harvard after Alpert admitted violating the agreement to not administer drugs to undergraduates. Leary continued his research with hallucinogens at a large estate in Millbrook, New York. He came to be seen as a controversial and charismatic rebel as he advocated both the therapeutic and recreational use of LSD—inviting people to "turn on, tune in, and drop

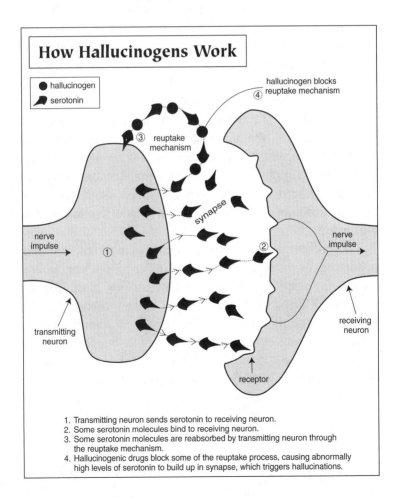

How Hallucinogens Work

1. Transmitting neuron sends serotonin to receiving neuron.
2. Some serotonin molecules bind to receiving neuron.
3. Some serotonin molecules are reabsorbed by transmitting neuron through the reuptake mechanism.
4. Hallucinogenic drugs block some of the reuptake process, causing abnormally high levels of serotonin to build up in synapse, which triggers hallucinations.

out." This invitation was attractive to the emerging hippie counterculture of the 1960s—a group comprised mainly of middle-class youths who challenged mainstream values by embracing communalism, free love, and alternative spirituality. They came to see taking hallucinogens—"turning on"—as a means to "tune in" to unrecognized dimensions of consciousness and "drop out" of a conformist worldview that had dominated American life for decades.

Up until 1965, there had been little press coverage on the use and spread of psychedelic drugs. However, the growing number of hippies migrating to San Francisco, New York, and other large cities began to draw media attention, and public concern about the dangers of hallucinogens grew. By 1966, articles and news stories focusing on the negative consequences of recreational drug use appeared in the mainstream media. An article in *Time* reported on the murder of a woman by her LSD-using son-in-law and the increase in hospital admissions due to LSD usage. Although fatal overdoses do not occur with most hallucinogens, a person high on LSD has seriously impaired judgment that can lead to dangerous actions. Even researcher Richard Alpert became convinced, after numerous LSD trips, that he could fly. His attempt to do so resulted in a broken leg.

The prospects for serious professional research involving hallucinogens dwindled as national anxiety about drug abuse increased. In April 1966, an amendment to the Drug Control Act made it illegal to manufacture or sell psychedelic drugs. Sandoz Laboratories, the patent holder of LSD and psilocybin, voluntarily turned over their entire supply to the FDA. In 1968, after reports had aired that LSD could cause chromosome damage and birth defects, possession of LSD became illegal. Two years later, Congress passed the Controlled Substances Act, which established a new classification system for drugs based on their potential for misuse. Thereafter, all drugs considered to have a high abuse potential and no accepted medical use were defined as Schedule I substances. Marijuana,

LSD, psilocybin, peyote, and mescaline were classified under Schedule I.

Between 1970 and 1990, experiments with hallucinogens were largely restricted to animal studies and harm assessment. Researchers were required to obtain rigorously guarded Schedule I licenses from the Drug Enforcement Administration (DEA). Its stringent rules made scientific research "difficult, if not impossible," explains psychedelic researcher Stanislav Grof. Moreover, scientists could find little institutional support for therapeutic research on hallucinogens. In Grof's opinion, this was because "the image of LSD was not shaped by already existing extensive professional literature; it was dictated by mass media sensationalizing the accidents of unsupervised self-experimentation and spreading scientifically unsubstantiated rumors about chromosome damage and genetic dangers."

In 1989 the FDA updated the approval process for research on investigational drugs. While scientists researching hallucinogens still must obtain special licenses from the DEA, several studies on the therapeutic potential of hallucinogens have recently been approved. Medical researcher Charles Grob, for example, began a study in 2003 that he believes will reveal the beneficial emotional effects of psilocybin on the terminally ill. In addition, psychiatrist Michael Mithoefer obtained approval in 2004 to conduct MDMA ("ecstasy")-assisted therapy sessions with victims of violence who are suffering from post-traumatic stress disorder.

By and large, hallucinogens remain illegal and controversial. As recent investigations indicate, however, some scientists may plan to challenge the Schedule I definition of these drugs as having "no accepted medical use." The future of hallucinogens is thus likely to be as complex and compelling as their history.

CHAPTER ONE

The Early History
of Hallucinogens

The Significance of Hallucinogens in Ancient Cultures

Richard Evans Schultes

Widely hailed as "the father of ethnobotany," Richard Evans Schultes was director of the Botanical Museum at Harvard University, where he also studied and taught courses in botany. Before his death in 2001, Schultes spent decades conducting research on the relationship between people and plants in the Americas. In this selection, Schultes discusses the significance of hallucinogenic plants to aboriginal societies and ancient cultures. Archaeological evidence and mythological studies reveal that hallucinogens played a major role in all aspects of primitive life. Religious beliefs and theories about the origins of the cosmos were deeply influenced by hallucinogenic plants, as ancient peoples believed that they granted access to spiritual forces and supernatural realms.

From his earliest gropings as a distinct animal, man undoubtedly experimented with his vegetal surroundings. He put into his stomach anything from the plant kingdom in his frantic search for nourishment. He early discovered that some plants served to assuage hunger and sustain him; others relieved symptoms of illness; still others were dangerous, making him ill or killing him outright; but a few, he found, transported him from this monotonous and not-too-pleasant mundane exis-

Richard Evans Schultes, "Plants and Plant Constituents as Mind-Altering Agents Throughout History," *Handbook of Psychopharmacology*, vol. 11, edited by Leslie L. Iversen, Susan B. Iversen, and Solomon H. Snyder. New York: Plenum Press, 1978.

tence to realms of ethereal wonder and inexplicable separation from everyday existence. He had discovered the narcotics, especially the hallucinogenic plants, capable of much more than activity on the physical body but able, through their psychoactivity on the central nervous system, to alter in ways most extraordinary the psyche and its relationship to the natural affairs of man.

Much of the experimentation that led man to his hallucinogens was very early. One of man's earliest cultigens, *Cannabis*, dates from well nigh the beginnings of agriculture in the Old World—10,000 years ago. Specimens of coca leaves have been found in mummy bundles in some of the very early graves of Peru, in sites too early even for maize. Peyote buttons have recently been recovered from dry caves in New Mexico, which have been dated at 4,000 years of age.

The Ubiquity of Hallucinogens

Material evidence of the use of plant products as hallucinogens is certainly not lacking in archaeological sites. Yet from the importance of hallucinogens in aboriginal mythology and religion we know that they have played roles so ancient that they are basic concepts even in the origin myths of peoples in primitive societies around the world. There has been the suggestion that one of the oldest hallucinogens—*Amanita muscaria*—may go back as a narcotic so far in man's prehistory that it engendered the notion of divinity and the supernatural.

It requires only a glance at beliefs surrounding some of the hallucinogens to appreciate their basic nature and significance to aboriginal concepts concerning the origin of man and his cultures: hence their great age. The fact that hallucinogens in many aboriginal societies permeate all aspects of living is evidence of their antiquity fully as convincing as material remains.

They reach into prenatal life and influence life after death; they operate throughout earthly existence. They play roles not only in health and sickness but in the relationships between individuals, villages, and tribes, in peace and war, at home and in travel, in hunting and in agriculture—there is hardly any aspect of living or dying where hallucinogenic plants do not play a major role.

It is not at all difficult to understand why hallucinogens have penetrated so deeply into all aspects of primitive societies. Man in primitive societies had to explain why a few plants possessed unearthly powers that could transfer him temporarily from everyday existence to realms of ethereal wonder. His explanation maintained that these plants were the abode of a divinity or spiritual force, and they became sacred. This concept, actually, is not wholly confined to so-called primitive societies, since many of the religions of the more advanced cultures are based on similar beliefs: witness the widespread Christian thesis that a divinity could incarnate itself into the body of a man, Jesus. But in societies based on the belief that all of nature is controlled by the supernatural, that all of man's existence—even sickness and death—is ruled by powers in outer realms, what is more logical than to assume

 THE HISTORY OF DRUGS

Awe and Terror

The origins of man's use of visionary, mind-changing plants and preparations [are] lost in the obscurities of prerecorded history. Perhaps some Neolithic shaman, sampling new specimens for his herbal pharmacopeia, stumbled across and ingested an innocuous-looking weed; in a short time, he found himself in the company of the tribal ancestors, spirits of water, thunder, rock and earth, trembling with stark awe and terror at the mysterious energies flashing through his eyes and ears, marveling at the intricacies of the relationships between man and animal, man and man, struggling with the subtle entrapments of his own fantastic concepts and visions.

Ralph Metzner, *The Ecstatic Adventure*, 1968.

that these plants enable mortal man—or at least certain individuals in society—to communicate through hallucinogens of various kinds with the ruling forces? As [anthropologist Weston] La Barre (1970) maintains: 'Sacred knowledge is commonly traceable, even by natives themselves, to an origin in revelation given to the ancestors or to some similarly charismatic individual, such as a shaman, visionary prophet or other culture hero believed to have been able to "tap" the unseen world of the "supernatural".'

There are many characteristics of hallucinations that can and do deeply influence primitive religion and ideas of the cosmos. Certain hallucinogenic plants—peyote, for example—induce indescribably deep and rich colours that are so unlike those normally experienced that only a supernatural origin seems possible; others produce only reds, oranges, or yellows; still others tend to be responsible for duller tones of blues, purples, or greys. The intoxication caused by some of these plants, especially those containing tryptamines, is characterized by macropsia and undoubtedly has played a role in mythology in connection with giants; others, however, have an opposite effect, micropsia, and have influenced belief—such as with the *oprita* of the Kofans—in the 'little people'. Other hallucinogens enable man to fly through the air by inducing the sense of levitation: shanshi of the Ecuadorian highlands; vinho de jurema in Brazil, the fly agaric in Siberia, the solanaceous species of medieval witches' brews of Europe.

Similarly, auditory hallucinations may enable medicine men and often others to speak with the controlling spirit forces: sinicuichi, gi-i-wa and gi-i-sa-wa, and thle-pela-kano in Mexico fall into this category. The peyote intoxication may, at certain phases, induce auditory aberrations and, like other hallucinogens such as *Cannabis*, may evoke peculiar response to chanting, singing, music, drumming, or natural sounds like that of rippling waters—an effect clearly suggesting in aboriginal thinking supernatural connections between the causative drug and man.

A Theory on Hallucinogens and Evolution

Terence McKenna

Born in 1946, Terence McKenna was an author, lecturer, and ethnopharmacologist who specialized in the study of psychoactive plants and shamanism. In 1985, McKenna cofounded Botanical Dimensions, a nonprofit organization that collects and distributes medicinal plants from the tropics. From the 1990s until his death from cancer in 2000, McKenna wrote and lectured widely on hallucinogenic plants and their influence on culture. His sometimes fantastic ideas and presentations have led some to dismiss his theories while others find him to be a bold, visionary thinker. In the following selection, excerpted from his book *Food of the Gods: The Search for the Original Tree of Knowledge*, McKenna presents his theory concerning the relationship between hallucinogenic plants and human evolution. According to McKenna, the psychoactive compounds in certain edible fungi and plants initiated biochemical and genetic processes that led to the emergence of language and religion.

The ways in which humans use plants, foods, and drugs cause the values of individuals and, ultimately, whole societies to shift. Eating some foods makes us happy, eating others sleepy, and still others alert. We are jovial, restless, aroused, or depressed depending on what we have eaten. Society tacitly encourages certain behaviors that correspond to internal feelings, thereby encouraging the use of substances that produce acceptable behaviors.

Suppression or expression of sexuality, fertility and sexual potency, degree of visual acuity, sensitivity to sound, speed of motor response, rate of maturation, and lifespan—these are only some of an animal's characteristics that can be influenced by food plants with exotic chemistries. Human symbol formation, linguistic facility, and sensitivity to community values may also shift under the influence of psychoactive and physiologically active metabolites. A night spent observing behavior in a singles bar should be fieldwork enough to confirm this observation. Indeed the mate-getting hustle has always placed a high premium on linguistic facility, as perennial attention to patter styles and opening lines attests.

When thinking about drugs, we tend to focus on episodes of intoxication, but many drugs are normally used in subthreshold or maintenance doses; coffee and tobacco are obvious examples in our culture. The result of this is a kind of "ambience of intoxication." Like fish in water, people in a culture swim in the virtually invisible medium of culturally sanctioned yet artificial states of mind.

Languages appear invisible to the people who speak them, yet they create the fabric of reality for their users. The problem of mistaking language for reality in the everyday world is only too well known. Plant use is an example of a complex language of chemical and social interactions. Yet most of us are unaware of the effects of plants on ourselves and our reality, partly because we have forgotten that plants have always mediated the human cultural relationship to the world at large.

A Shaggy Primate Story

At Gombe Stream National Park in Tanzania, primatologists found that one particular species of leaf kept appearing undigested in chimpanzee dung. They found that every few days the chimps, instead of eating wild fruit as usual, would walk for twenty minutes or more to a site where a species of *Aspilia* grew. The chimps would repeatedly place their lips over an *Aspilia* leaf and hold it in their mouths. They would pluck a leaf, place it in their mouths, roll it around for a few moments, then swallow it whole. In this way as many as thirty small leaves might be eaten.

Biochemist Eloy Rodriguez of the University of California at Irvine isolated the active principle from the *Aspilia*—a reddish oil now named thiarubrine-A. Nell Towers of the University of British Columbia found that this compound can kill common bacteria in concentrations of less than one part per million. Herbarium records studied by Rodriguez and Towers showed that African peoples used *Aspilia* leaves to treat wounds and stomachaches. Of the four species native to Africa, the indigenous peoples used only three, the same three species used by the chimpanzees.

Rodriguez and Towers have continued their observations of chimp and plant interactions and can now identify nearly a dozen plants, a veritable materia medica, in use among chimpanzee populations.

You Are What You Eat

Our proposed story of human emergence into the light of self-reflection is a you-are-what-you-eat story. Major climatic change and a newly broadened and hence mutagenic diet provided many opportunities for natural selection to affect the evolution of major human traits. Each encounter with a new food, drug, or flavoring was fraught with risk and unpredictable consequences. And this is even more true today, when our food contains hundreds of poorly studied preservatives and additives.

As an example of plants with a potential impact on a human population, consider sweet potatoes of the genus *Dioscorea*. In much of the tropical world, sweet potatoes provide a reliable and nutritious source of food. Nevertheless, several closely related species contain compounds that can interfere with ovulation. (These have become the source of raw materials for modern birth control pills.) Something close to genetic chaos would descend on a population of primates that settled into feeding upon these species of *Dioscorea*. Many such scenarios, though of a less spectacular magnitude, must have occurred as early hominids experimented with new foods while expanding their omnivorous dietary habits.

Eating a plant or an animal is a way of claiming its power, a way of assimilating its magic to one's self. In the minds of preliterate people, the lines between drugs, foods, and spices are rarely clearly drawn. The shaman who gorges himself on chili peppers to raise inner heat is hardly in a less altered state than the nitrous oxide enthusiast after a long inhalation. In our perception of flavor and our pursuit of variety in the sensation of eating, we are markedly different from even our primate cousins. Somewhere along the line, our new omnivorous eating habits and our evolving brain with its capacity to process sensory data were united in the happy notion that food can be experience. Gastronomy was born—born to join pharmacology, which must surely have preceded it, since maintenance of health through regulation of diet is seen among many animals.

The strategy of the early hominid omnivores was to eat everything that seemed foodlike and to vomit whatever was unpalatable. Plants, insects, and small animals found edible by this method were then inculcated into their diet. A changing diet or an omnivorous diet means exposure to an ever-shifting chemical equilibrium. An organism may regulate this chemical input through internal processes but, ultimately, mutagenic influences will increase and a greater than usual number of genetically variant individuals will be offered up to the process of natural selection. The results of this natural selection are accelerated changes in neural organization, states of consciousness, and behavior. No change is permanent, each gives way to yet another. All flows. . . .

A New View of Human Evolution

The first encounters between hominids and psilocybin-containing mushrooms may have predated the domestication of cattle in Africa by a million years or more. And during this million-year period, the mushrooms were not only gathered and eaten but probably also achieved the status of a cult. But domestication of wild cattle, a great step in human cultural evolution, by bringing humans into greater proximity to cattle, also entailed increased contact with the mushrooms, because these mushrooms grow only in the dung of cattle. As a result, the human-mushroom interspecies codependency was enhanced and deepened. It was at this time that religious ritual, calendar making, and natural magic came into their own. . . .

In pondering the course of human evolution, some thoughtful observers have questioned the scenario that physical anthropologists present us. Evolution in higher animals takes a long time to occur, operating in time spans of rarely less than a million years and more often in tens of millions of years. But the emergence of modern humans from the higher primates—with the enormous changes effected in brain size and behavior—transpired in fewer than three million years. Physically, in the last 100,000 years, we have apparently changed very little. But the amazing proliferation of cultures, social institutions, and linguistic systems has come so quickly that modern evolutionary biologists can scarcely account for it. Most do not even attempt an explanation.

Indeed, the absence of a theoretical model is not surprising; there is much that we do not know about the complex situation prevailing among the hominids just prior to and during the time when modern human beings were emerging onto the scene. Biological and fossil evidence clearly indicates that man is descended from primate ancestors not radically different from primate species still extant, and yet *Homo sapiens* obviously is in a class apart from other members of the order.

Thinking about human evolution ultimately means thinking about the evolution of human consciousness. What, then, are the origins of the human mind? In their explanations, some investigators have adopted a primarily cultural emphasis. They point to our unique linguistic and symbolical capabilities, our use of tools, and our ability to store information epigenetically as songs, art, books, computers, thereby creating not only culture, but also history. Others, taking a somewhat more biological approach, have emphasized our physiological and neurological peculiarities, including the exceptionally large size and complexity of the human neocortex, a great proportion of which is devoted to complex linguistic processing, storage, and retrieval of information, as well as being associated with motor systems governing activities like speech and writing. More recently the feedback interactions between cultural influence and biological ontogeny have been recognized and seen to be involved in certain human developmental oddities, such as prolonged childhood and adolescence, the delayed onset of sexual maturity, and the persistence of many essentially neonatal characteristics through adult life. Unfortunately the union of these points of view has not yet led to the recognition of the genome-shaping power of psychoactive and physioactive dietary constituents. . . .

The Real Missing Link

My contention is that mutation-causing, psychoactive chemical compounds in the early human diet directly influenced the rapid reorganization of the brain's information-processing capacities. Alkaloids in plants, specifically the hallucinogenic compounds such as psilocybin, dimethyltryptamine (DMT), and harmaline, could be the chemical factors in the protohuman diet that catalyzed the emergence of human self-reflection. The action of hallucinogens present in many common plants enhanced our information-processing activity, or environmental sensitivity, and thus contributed to the sudden expansion of the human brain size. At a later stage in this same process, hallucinogens acted as catalysts in the develop-

ment of imagination, fueling the creation of internal strata-
gems and hopes that may well have synergized the emergence
of language and religion.

In research done in the late 1960s, Roland Fischer gave
small amounts of psilocybin to graduate students and then
measured their ability to detect the moment when previously
parallel lines became skewed. He found that performance ability on this particular task was actually improved after small
doses of psilocybin.

When I discussed these findings with Fischer, he smiled after explaining his conclusions, then summed up, "You see
what is conclusively proven here is that under certain circumstances one is actually better informed concerning the real
world if one has taken a drug than if one has not." His face-
tious remark stuck with me, first as an academic anecdote,
later as an effort on his part to communicate something profound. What would be the consequences for evolutionary theory of admitting that some chemical habits confer adaptive advantage and thereby become deeply scripted in the behavior
and even genome of some individuals?

Three Big Steps for the Human Race

In trying to answer that question I have constructed a scenario,
some may call it fantasy; it is the world as seen from the vantage point of a mind for which the millennia are but seasons, a
vision that years of musing on these matters has moved me toward. Let us imagine for a moment that we stand outside the
surging gene swarm that is biological history, and that we can
see the interwoven consequences of changes in diet and climate, which must certainly have been too slow to be felt by our
ancestors. The scenario that unfolds involves the intercon-
nected and mutually reinforcing effects of psilocybin taken at
three different levels. Unique in its properties, psilocybin is the
only substance, I believe, that could yield this scenario.

At the first, low, level of usage is the effect that Fischer

noted: small amounts of psilocybin, consumed with no awareness of its psychoactivity while in the general act of browsing
for food, and perhaps later consumed consciously, impart a
noticeable increase in visual acuity, especially edge detection.
As visual acuity is at a premium among hunter-gatherers, the
discovery of the equivalent of "chemical binoculars" could not
fail to have an impact on the hunting and gathering success of
those individuals who availed themselves of this advantage.
Partnership groups containing individuals with improved eyesight will be more successful at feeding their offspring. Because of the increase in available food, the offspring within
such groups will have a higher probability of themselves
reaching reproductive age. In such a situation, the outbreeding
(or decline) of non-psilocybin-using groups would be a natural
consequence.

Because psilocybin is a stimulant of the central nervous
system, when taken in slightly larger doses, it tends to trigger
restlessness and sexual arousal. Thus, at this second level of
usage, by increasing instances of copulation, the mushrooms
directly favored human reproduction. The tendency to regulate
and schedule sexual activity within the group, by linking it to
a lunar cycle of mushroom availability, may have been important as a first step toward ritual and religion. Certainly at the
third and highest level of usage, religious concerns would be at
the forefront of the tribe's consciousness, simply because of
the power and strangeness of the experience itself.

This third level, then, is the level of the full-blown shamanic
ecstasy. The psilocybin intoxication is a rapture whose
breadth and depth is the despair of prose. It is wholly Other
and no less mysterious to us than it was to our mushroom-
munching ancestors. The boundary-dissolving qualities of
shamanic ecstasy predispose hallucinogen-using tribal groups
to community bonding and to group sexual activities, which
promote gene mixing, higher birth rates, and a communal
sense of responsibility for the group offspring.

At whatever dose the mushroom was used, it possessed the

magical property of conferring adaptive advantages upon its archaic users and their group. Increased visual acuity, sexual arousal, and access to the transcendent Other led to success in obtaining food, sexual prowess and stamina, abundance of offspring, and access to realms of supernatural power. All of these advantages can be easily self-regulated through manipulation of dosage and frequency of ingestion. . . . Its power is so extraordinary that psilocybin can be considered the catalyst to the human development of language.

Responding to Objections

An objection to these ideas inevitably arises and should be dealt with. This scenario of human emergence may seem to smack of Lamarckism, which theorizes that characteristics acquired by an organism during its lifetime can be passed on to its progeny. The classic example is the claim that giraffes have long necks because they stretch their necks to reach high branches. This straightforward and rather common-sense idea is absolutely anathema among neo-Darwinians, who currently hold the high ground in evolutionary theory. Their position is that mutations are entirely random and that only after the mutations are expressed as the traits of organisms does natural selection mindlessly and dispassionately fulfill its function of preserving those individuals upon whom an adaptive advantage had been conferred.

Their objection can be put like this: While the mushrooms may have given us better eyesight, sex, and language when eaten, how did these enhancements get into the human genome and become innately human? Nongenetic enhancements of an organism's functioning made by outside agents retard the corresponding genetic reservoirs of those facilities by rendering them superfluous. In other words, if a necessary metabolite is common in available food, there will not be pressure to develop a trait for endogenous expression of the metabolite. Mushroom use would thus create individuals with less visual acuity, language facility, and consciousness. Nature would not provide those enhancements through organic evolution because the metabolic investment required to sustain them wouldn't pay off, relative to the tiny metabolic investment required to eat mushrooms. And yet today we all have these enhancements, without taking mushrooms. So how did the mushroom modifications get into the genome?

The short answer to this objection, one that requires no defense of [French naturalist Jean-Baptiste] Lamarck's ideas, is that the presence of psilocybin in the hominid diet changed the parameters of the process of natural selection by changing the behavioral patterns upon which that selection was operating. Experimentation with many types of foods was causing a general increase in the numbers of random mutations being offered up to the process of natural selection, while the augmentation of visual acuity, language use, and ritual activity through the use of psilocybin represented new behaviors. One of these new behaviors, language use, previously only a marginally important trait, was suddenly very useful in the context of new hunting and gathering lifestyles. Hence psilocybin inclusion in the diet shifted the parameters of human behavior in favor of patterns of activity that promoted increased language; acquisition of language led to more vocabulary and an expanded memory capacity. The psilocybin-using individuals evolved epigenetic rules or cultural forms that enabled them to survive and reproduce better than other individuals. Eventually the more successful epigenetically based styles of behavior spread through the populations along with the genes that reinforce them. In this fashion the population would evolve genetically and culturally.

From Ancient Rites to Flower Power: The Story of Ergot

Joan W. Bennett and Roland Bentley

In the following essay, Joan W. Bennett and Roland Bentley discuss the history of ergot, a toxic and hallucinogenic substance found in a fungus that grows on rye. When eaten in its unrefined form, ergot can cause a painful contraction of blood vessels, bizarre behavior, convulsions, gangrene, brain damage, and death. Ergot poisoning afflicted many northern European communities during the Middle Ages, the authors point out. By the sixteenth and seventeenth centuries, midwives were using extracts of ergot to induce abortions and to hasten childbirth—although such usage was often forbidden because of its inherent dangers. In the twentieth century, scholars theorized that ergot may have been the hallucinogenic agent used in certain ancient Greek mystical ceremonies; some also speculated that ergot poisoning may have been the source of the panic that led to the Salem witch trials in 1691. Currently, LSD is the most well-known ergot derivative. Before it became associated with the counterculture of the 1960s, LSD was the subject of serious intellectual inquiry and psychiatric research, the authors explain. Bennett is a professor in the department of cell and molecular biology at Tulane University in New Orleans, Louisiana. Bentley is an emeritus professor with the department of biological sciences at the University of Pittsburgh in Pennsylvania.

Joan W. Bennett and Roland Bentley, "Pride and Prejudice: The Story of Ergot," *Perspectives in Biology and Medicine*, vol. 42, March 22, 1999, p. 333. Copyright © 1999 by the Johns Hopkins University Press. Reproduced by permission.

For thousands of years, healers and physicians relied on plant extracts for curative purposes, unwittingly utilizing the pharmacological properties of the chemical constituents they contained. Belladonna (atropine), digitalis, opium, quinine, and salicylic acid have been used in crude form since antiquity, and their Janus-faced qualities provided the first lessons in the vagaries of drug action. Opium relieved pain but also caused stupor, addiction, and death. Overdoses of digitalis could be lethal. Not surprisingly, supernatural causes were regularly invoked to explain the potent and unpredictable effects of botanical medicinals. . . .

This article discusses a historically fascinating group of natural products from fungi—the ergot alkaloids. Arguably the oldest of the microbial biopharmaceutins [natural medicinal products], they may have played a role in both the Mysteries of Eleusis [in ancient Greece] and the Salem Witch trials. Used by midwives for centuries, they were among the first effective obstetric drugs. Best known for their toxic and psychoactive effects, they also figured prominently in tales of medieval pestilence. Ergot poisoning following the ingestion of contaminated grains was characterized by burning sensations caused by the contraction of blood vessels. The pain was likened to a "fire," and the fire was described as divine, sacred, or occult. Sufferers prayed to the Virgin Mary or St. Anthony for intercession. Sometimes ergot poisoning was accompanied by hallucinations and bizarre behavior, symptoms that could be interpreted as bewitchment or possession by the devil.

The physiological effects of ergot reflected not only the concentrations and combinations of the ingested ergot metabolites, but also the age and nutritional status of the individual who consumed them. Just as importantly, the sociological interpretation of the ergot response reflected the cultural milieu in which it was encountered. Sufferers were pitied or persecuted, depending on whether they were perceived as the targets or the perpetrators of witchcraft. Eventually an array of pharmacologically potent ergot alkaloids was purified from a single fungal structure, the sclerotium. Only within the last few decades has it been possible to take pride in the limited and careful use of ergot products in medicine (e.g., for the treatment of migraine and to assuage postpartum hemorrhage). Research on medicinal alkaloids led to the serendipitous discovery of lysergic acid diethylamide (LSD), which was followed by a brief era of legitimate research on hallucinogens.

Ergot and Ergotism

As civilizations developed and records were kept, many catastrophic diseases were described with enough detail to permit retrospective diagnosis. In the Middle Ages, the Black Death (bubonic plague) was among the most famous. [British prime minister] Winston Churchill provides a vivid description: "The character of the pestilence was appalling. The disease itself, with its frightful symptoms, the swift onset, the blotches, the hardening of the glands under the armpit or in the groin, these swellings which no poultice could resolve, these tumours which, when lanced, gave no relief, the horde of virulent carbuncles which followed the dread harbingers of death, the delirium, the insanity which attended its triumph, the blank spaces which opened on all sides in human society, stunned and for a time destroyed the life of the world. This affliction, added to all the severities of the Middle Ages, was more than the human spirit could endure."

While less well known than the Black Death, another affliction of the Middle Ages was the disease now known as ergotism. Bubonic plague was contagious, spread by the bites of rat fleas and caused by the bacterium Yersinia pestis. In sharp contrast, ergotism was not infectious but was caused by the ingestion of toxic fungal metabolites contaminating the food supply, usually rye. In northern Europe, especially before the introduction of the potato, the dependence of the population on rye flour meant that ergotism could be as destructive to a community as was the Black Death. In modern terminology, ergotism is the earliest recorded instance of a mycotoxicosis (i.e., a poisoning caused by mold toxins).

The fungus mainly responsible for the production of ergot alkaloids is *Claviceps purpurea*, a species which parasitizes rye as well as other cereals and grains. *Claviceps* has a complex, three-stage life cycle. Spores alight on rye flowers, germinate, and produce hyphae which destroy the young ovary of the rye, eventually forming a hard, seed-like structure termed the sclerotium. Sclerotia of *C. purpurea* have a dark violet or black color and are somewhat larger than the rye grains (about 1 to 5 cm long). They fall to the ground where they over-winter before germination occurs, spores form, and the cycle begins again. Sclerotia are easily recognized; one mycologist has described how he "picked more than a teaspoonful from a pound of wild rice bought at a trading post."

The sclerotia are known as ergots, or more specifically as ergots of rye. The word derives from Old French, argot, and French, ergot, used to describe the shape of a cock's spur, which a sclerotium resembles. . . .

A Disease of Antiquity

Cold, wet weather favors the growth of the fungus, with the worst outbreaks following a severe winter succeeded by a rainy spring. The ergots contain a cocktail of toxic alkaloids that are retained in flour after the milling of contaminated grain. Typically, ergotism in humans arises from consumption of bread, especially that made from rye. The alkaloids have considerable stability and survive both baking and boiling.

Clinicians distinguish two forms of ergotism: gangrenous and convulsive. In the gangrenous form, the toxic alkaloids restrict blood flow, leading to many grotesque symptoms. One characteristic is a swelling of the limbs with alternate sensations of fiery heat and cold. There may be tingling and itching in the skin, a condition known as formication. Eventually, a dry gangrene afflicts nails, fingers, toes, and limbs. The extremities become black; in severe cases the mummified parts become separated from the body with no loss of blood. In convulsive ergotism there are muscle spasms and "fits" or "convulsions," as well as massive nervous dysfunctions. Between convulsions, the victims suffer from insomnia and have voracious appetites. Those that survive may be mentally impaired.

Hallucinations, delusions, confusions, and a temporary or permanent psychosis may accompany either type of ergotism. The young, especially teenagers, are particularly affected. Moreover, ingestion of ergot by pregnant women can lead to abortion. The gangrenous form was common in France and west of the Rhine, whereas in Russia the convulsive form predominated. Inadequate nutrition almost certainly exacerbated cases of ergotism. Vitamin A deficiency due to lack of dairy products may have been particularly significant. . . .

Although ergotism is almost certainly a disease of great antiquity, the first clear-cut clinical descriptions do not appear until the 16th century. Prior to that time, there are many descriptions of pestilence which have the ring of ergotism. An Assyrian tablet (circa 600 BC) described a "noxious pustule in the ear of grain," and in sacred books of the Parsees (400–300 BC) are described "noxious grasses that cause pregnant women to drop the womb and die in childbed.". . .

The burning sensations of convulsive ergotism and the blackened limbs of the gangrenous form were attributed to some kind of "fire." Both were caused by the vasoconstrictive properties of the ergot alkaloids. In the absence of any detailed medical knowledge it was natural for deeply religious people to seek the help of saints and of the Virgin Mary. The most important of at least a dozen saints became St. Anthony (d. 356). He was born in Egypt, but after his death his remains were carried to France. During his lifetime he acquired a reputation for instantaneous cures and after his death he continued to be venerated: after a cure of "holy fire" attributed to him about 1090, ergotism came to be called St. Anthony's fire. A hospital brotherhood was founded and may actually have provided some relief, if only in the form of improved nutrition. . . .

Ergot and Obstetrics

It seems certain that in the 16th and 17th centuries, midwives used ergot during delivery, and by the 18th century there were written accounts of its use in obstetrics. Perhaps the first recorded recognition of ergot's oxytocic[1] activity occurred in 1787, when it was reported that it had been introduced into some pharmacies 30 years earlier "by an empiricist from the Netherlands" and was called *pulvis ad partum*. It is clear that ergot was used by European midwives in the 18th century and was sometimes forbidden by officials. It entered into medical records in the United States in 1808, when Dr. John Stearns of Saratoga County wrote a letter which was published in the Medical Repository of New York. Stearns recommended an ergot preparation, "*Pulvis parturiens*," to facilitate the work of accoucheurs [male obstetricians] noting with brutal frankness that since he began use of this ergot preparation, "I have seldom found a case that detained me more than three hours." By 1824, this use of ergot was correlated with an increase in the number of stillborn children. Noting the name, "*pulvis ad partum*," [scientist and physician David] Hosack suggested that as far as the child was concerned, "*pulvis ad mortem*" was more appropriate. . . .

Almost certainly midwives used extracts of ergot not only to precipitate childbirth but also to induce abortions. In either case, dosages were impossible to control, and use of these drugs was dangerous for both pregnant women and the midwives who administered them—the line between wise woman and witch was easily traversed: "Midwives were the victims of a vicious syllogism. To know the secrets was to be a witch; it was necessary to know the secrets to be a midwife; therefore, a midwife is a witch." Later, especially in the extreme anti-abortion climate of the late 19th century, the demonstrable efficacy of folk medicines such as ergot provided another reason to exclude and stigmatize the women who worked outside the

1. An oxytocic drug hastens childbirth by stimulating contractions of the uterus.

medical establishment. Contemporary furor over RU-486, a more dependable and less toxic substance than ergot, illustrates the depth of disapproval against abortion in general, and efficacious non-surgical abortion in particular.

Nevertheless, the ergot alkaloids were eventually embraced by obstetricians, not as abortifacients but as drugs to initiate or accelerate parturition [labor] and to assuage postpartum hemorrhage. The uterotonic effects of ergonovine and its semi-synthetic derivatives made these drugs popular in the first half of the 20th century. However, they often intensified uterine pain and caused serious side effects. Although still used after delivery to assist involution of the uterus and decrease hemorrhage, they have been largely replaced by oxytocin. . . .

Eleusinian Mysteries

Hallucinogenic ergot alkaloids may have had a major role in mystical ceremonies carried out in Ancient Greece for nearly 2,000 years. The ceremonies were held at Eleusis, a town near Athens, and thus were referred to as the Eleusinian Mysteries. The rite involved a symbolic reenactment of the story of the goddess Demeter, the earth mother whose only daughter Persephone was abducted to Hades. In autumn, new initiates participated in a sacramental ceremony, part of which involved a special drink. They experienced ecstatic visions, sometimes accompanied by trembling, vertigo, nausea, and a cold sweat. For those lucky enough to partake, it was said to be the supreme experience of a lifetime. The Greek poet Pindar wrote: "Happy is he who, having seen these rites, goes below the hollow earth; for he knows the end of life and he knows its god-sent beginning."

Participants in the Mysteries were pledged to silence—it was a capital offence to reveal what happened or what was consumed. Even without the mandatory secrecy, the experience was said to be ineffable—beyond the power of words to describe. As pilgrims reenacted the myth, they were transported to a state of transcendence and saw the spirit of Persephone surrounded by an aura of brilliant light. A definitive account was given by Gordon Wasson, Albert Hofmann, and Carl Ruck. Wasson, an amateur ethnomycologist, had discovered and publicized the shamanistic "magic" mushroom ceremonies in southern Mexico; he was intrigued by perceived similarities between the Eleusinian mysteries and the Mexican religious rites. Albert Hofmann was the chemist who had first synthesized LSD and unwittingly discovered its psychoactive properties, and finally, Carl Ruck was a Greek scholar. In their book, Ruck noted: "Since the sight could be offered to thousands of initiates each year dependably upon schedule, it seems obvious that an hallucinogen must have induced it." In addition to the knowledge that an elixir was consumed prior to the visual experience, several lines of evidence supported the hypothesis that ergot was involved: grain was an important part of the Eleusinian harvest festival; purple, the color of Demeter's robe, may signify the purple color of sclerotia; and small religious vessels adorned with barley ears in relief have been discovered in Minoan Crete. Moreover, there was a record of a scandalous security breach: certain aristocratic trend-setting Athenians celebrated the Mystery at home with intoxicated guests.

The secrecy of the Greek celebrants, and the later suppression of the ceremonies by the early Christians (one of whom was purported to say "that in this pagan rite there was materialized a stalk of barley") means that we have only fragmented records of what actually happened at Eleusis, and only an inferential case can be made that the mysterious Eleusinian potion was an extract of ergot, perhaps some kind of hallucinogenic beer. In contrast to ergotamine and related compounds, the hallucinogenic alkaloids are water-soluble. Thus, it would have been technically feasible for the Eleusinian priests to extract bioactive metabolites, although large quantities of sclerotia and considerable effort would have been required to prepare sufficient hallucinogen for consumption by hundreds of people. Apparently Wasson, Hofmann, and Ruck did not attempt to reproduce the sclerotial elixir for self-experimentation, and there are other hallucinogenic agents that could have been used by the ancient Greeks. Nevertheless, the ergot–Eleusinian Mystery hypothesis is tantalizing, and it is supported by much circumstantial evidence.

The Salem Witch Trials

Another curious question about ergot alkaloids has been raised in connection with the witch trials in Salem, Massachusetts, in 1691 to 1692. Many historians have been perplexed by this anomalous and tragic episode in Puritan history. Writing during the 1970s, a provocative hypothesis based on physiology was suggested by L. Caporael and later extended by M.K. Matossian—specifically, that the panic was essentially an outbreak of convulsive ergotism. The "afflicted" individuals, mainly teenage women and children, were often stricken with convulsive fits, and they described the activities of invisible "specters" and "familiars." They attributed their problems to the actions of "witches"—often seemingly well-respected members of the community (one was a former minister). Of those accused of witchcraft, 19 were hanged and one was pressed to death (there is a vivid reconstruction in the movie version of Arthur Miller's play, *The Crucible*). All of those executed stoutly maintained their innocence. Caporael believed that she had been able to match many of the symptoms of those bewitched with the symptoms of ergotism. For example, in addition to "fits" and hallucinations, the afflicted had the sense of being pinched, pricked, or bitten. There were also unexplained animal deaths.

The conclusions of Caporael and Matossian have been challenged by [scholars] N.P. Spanos and J. Gottlieb. A systematic examination of legal depositions of witnesses against the accused led to the conclusion that none of the persons for whom clinical profiles were available had the particular collection of symptoms characteristic of convulsive ergotism. The critics rejected the ergot hypothesis and concluded that the crisis at Salem was just a "typical" episode of witchcraft and "can be interpreted much more plausibly in terms of political and economic considerations that operated in Salem at that time."

Whether or not ergot poisoning precipitated the communal hysteria in Salem, it could only have done so in a certain social milieu, and the reservations of Spanos and Gottlieb are well taken. The environment and mindset of the individuals examining these historical data are also worth noting. It surely is not accidental that the hypotheses concerning both the Eleusian Mysteries and the Salem Witches were formulated during a time when there was widespread recreational use and media coverage of LSD and other hallucinogens. . . .

"Turn On. Tune In. Drop Out."

While 20th-century surveillance of agricultural products turned ergotism into largely a historical curiosity, by mid-century the most famous ergot derivative was making history of its own. Moving from "elitist" experimentation into the common culture, many would say that LSD created a modern pestilence, perhaps with greater societal impact than medieval ergotism. Timothy Leary, a former lecturer in clinical psychology at Harvard, became the high priest of the psychedelic movement. Leary was a master of the sound bite—long before it was called that—and rapidly became a celebrity proselytizer: "The only hope is dope"; LSD "turns you on to God"; "causes peace to break out"; allows women to "have several hundred orgasms" in a single session; "cures alcoholism"; and, more ironically, "is so powerful that one administered dose can start a thousand rumors." A great deal has been written about this tumultuous epoch and the role played by Leary and psychedelic drugs. To greatly oversimplify, in the minds of many conservative Americans Leary came to represent the whole counterculture of "hippie freaks," and LSD came to represent the key catalyst of social and cultural unrest.

Today, mention of psychedelic drugs evokes this counter-culture of hippies, flower children, and anti-war protest. However, there was a time when LSD was the subject of scholarly papers, academic symposia, and serious psychiatric research. Greeted as something of a wonder drug by the psychiatric profession in the 1950s, a voluminous literature developed. LSD was used to treat conditions ranging from memory loss and frigidity through schizophrenia and the pain associated with terminal cancer, and was considered particularly efficacious in combating alcoholism. Two books that appeared in 1967 provide a window on that era of medically sanctioned clinical research: *The Use of LSD in Psychotherapy and Alcoholism* and *The Hallucinogens*. Many believed that of all the mind-altering drugs, hallucinogens such as LSD had the lowest potential for abuse. Psychologically potent in very low concentrations, even huge overdoses weren't lethal—although they could cause "bad trips." Intellectuals such as Aldous Huxley studied LSD as a way to enhance consciousness, theologians and divinity students respected the capacity of psychedelic agents to recreate the transcendent experiences of saints and religious mystics, and anthropologists sought clues to plant extracts used by native populations to "talk to their gods." In one of the loonier chapters of American history, as part of a program called Operation MK-ULTRA, the CIA even investigated the potential of LSD as a truth serum for use in interrogating enemy agents.

The crackdown began in 1962, when the Food and Drug Administration (FDA) designated LSD an "experimental drug" so that scientists needed special permission to do research on it. Congress passed the Drug Abuse Control Amendments in 1965, further tightening restrictions, and Sandoz [Laboratories] stopped marketing in 1966. The non-medical sale of LSD became a felony in 1968, and in 1970 it was placed in the Schedule I category of the Bureau of Narcotics and Dangerous Drugs, a classification for drugs of abuse with no medicinal value. Accompanying these restrictions were frightening and negative editorials in the *Journal of the American Medical Associ-*

ation and a media campaign emphasizing and exaggerating the ominous consequences of psychedelics: LSD was said to precipitate psychosis, drive users to suicide, and taint the gene pool through chromosome breakage. LSD had undeniably unpredictable and profound psychological effects, but the publicity crusade went beyond legitimate scientific concerns and was filled with misinformation. Perhaps the reaction was more against the way LSD threatened traditional values than against the way it threatened public health. . . .

Aided by advances in genomics, combinatorial chemistry, and other technological innovation, the search for new and better drugs goes on. The ambiguous legacy of ergot demonstrates that the most promising new biopharmaceutins are likely, by their very nature, to have unexpected consequences that extend beyond the pharmacy.

The Witches' Brews of Medieval Europe

Paul Devereux

The so-called "witches' brews" of medieval Europe were actually ointments enriched with hallucinogenic herbs, contends Paul Devereux in the following selection. Practitioners of traditional healing and magical arts—defined as "witches" by the church—concocted such potions as part of an ancient ritual known as night traveling. Night travelers would smear the ointment on their bodies, and occasionally on rods or staffs that they would place between their legs, Devereux explains. They would then have hallucinations of flying across the countryside and into the wilderness. The mythical image of the witch flying on a broomstick is derived from the hallucinations of the night travelers, Devereux notes. Devereux is a writer and researcher who specializes in the study of ancient sites and the study of consciousness.

The magical and medicinal plant lore of the rural "wise woman" (or man) in Anglo-Saxon, medieval, and immediately postmedieval Europe may not occupy a period we can properly call prehistory, but we can say that it was *outside* history in that it was a living knowledge largely overlooked or dismissed by the ruling classes and the sophisticates, or discouraged and repressed by the Church. The Church-orchestrated witch persecutions of the late Middle Ages and the century immediately after the medieval era transformed what was in fact a quietly surviving country tradition into what was hysterically and neurotically seen as a satanic activity. This distortion fed the needs of the Church. The remnants of these ancient traditions of plant lore survived in fragmented form and endure in isolated pockets to this day, especially in eastern Europe and the western Celtic fringe of the continent.

Night Travelers

One of the key elements of what became known as "witch lore" was that witches were able to fly on broomsticks, rods, or other instruments to their sabbats and other nighttime gatherings, held in the dark woods beyond the pale of the town. "Flying ointments" were often used, either smeared on the person's body or flying implements. Long before the Church contextualized this "flying out" to the wilderness as a diabolic practice, however, it was simply a part of the practice of women and men wise in the rural magic arts and healing based on arcane plant knowledge. The people who became identified as "witches" by the Church were in actuality simply the practitioners of an ancient tradition—"night travelers." In northern Europe they were called *qveldriga*, "night rider," or *myrkrida*, "rider in the dark." In Scandinavia, there was the tradition of *seidhr*, in which a prophetess or *seidhonka* would travel to farmsteads and hamlets with a group of girls to give divinatory trance sessions. She wore a ritual costume and carried a staff. The goddess Freya, who taught Odin the secrets of magical flight, was the patron of *seidhr*, and is shown in a twelfth-century mural in Schleswig cathedral, Germany, in the cloak of a *seidhonka* flying on a distaff. Her sister, or alternate aspect, Frigg, accompanies her, flying on a large striped cat. "Night travellers and the later witches are carelessly lumped together," [anthopologist] Hans Peter Duerr warns.

Depending on the time or place in Europe they operated, the night travelers might join the flying hosts of Diana, or Frau Holda—Mother Holle, the Old Norse Hela—the veiled goddess of the underworld, whose sacred bird was the migrant snow goose.[1] She is remembered in the nursery-rhyme image of Old Mother Goose, who, when she wanted to wander, we will recall, would fly through the air on a very fine gander. Researcher Nigel Jackson has noted:

> Celtic iconography from the Dauphine shows the goddess Epona riding upon a goose in flight. The high calls of the migrant geese on winter nights were poetically perceived as the baying of the spectral hounds by folk in the north of Europe and are closely linked with the flight of the Wild Hunt in Celtic and Germanic regions. The German witch Agnes Gerhardt said at her trial in 1596 that she and her companions transformed themselves into snow-geese in order to fly to the sabbat.

Medieval "witches" sometimes rubbed themselves with goose grease, perhaps enriched with hallucinogenic herbs, as a symbolic gesture of supernatural flight. Duerr remarks that the night flights were known as "grease flights" and the night travelers themselves were called "grease birds" or "lard wings."

The antiquity of the image of the night-flying woman is shown by such instances as the scene in *The Golden Ass*, written by Lucius Apuleius in the second century A.D., in which a woman is seen smearing herself all over with an ointment, muttering a charm, turning into an owl, and flying off over the rooftops. The night traveler and later the "witch" surely represented the vestiges of archaic Indo-European shamanism: she is the last echo of traditional ecstatic experience in Europe, an echo the Church effectively silenced by intimidation, widespread persecution, and sheer murder.

Civilization Versus Wilderness

The boundary between the town or village ("civilization") and the wilderness beyond was freighted with dark meaning in

---

1. The winter snows were said to be feathers falling from these birds' wings. (The goose or gander was a widespread symbol of shamanic spirit flight, ranging from the iconography of Siberian shamans to the literature of Vedic India to archaeological finds of geese effigies in the graves of Inuit—Eskimo—shamans.)

medieval Europe. Jackson points out that Saxon tribes referred to the night traveler as *haegtessa*, the "hedge rider," for she could traverse the mysterious "hedge" (boundary) that divided the worlds of the living and the dead. "Very early, women undertaking 'night travels' and fence demons are mentioned in the same breath," Duerr informs. The stick on which the woman rode was known as a "fence switch." The idea of the hedge-hopping night traveler or witch took on literal meaning in the minds of the ordinary people, and plants such as juniper, thought to ward off witches, were woven into real, physical hedges. Certain places along hedgerows were thought to be where witches were able to breach the boundary. The front doors of houses would be protected by such devices as "witch bottles," tangled threads inside a bottle that would ensnare the spirit of any night-traveling witch who might happen to gain entry.

The real boundary was that between the conscious, waking mind—"civilization"—and the dark, fearsome, and unknown regions of the unconscious—"wilderness." It was simply literalized and projected onto the physical environment. In reality, the night traveler's flight into the wilderness was, of course, a trance "journey" into the deep reaches of the unconscious mind, a "spirit flight" caused, usually, by hallucinogens in the flying ointments. The woman herself might even think of it as being a literal flight: John Cotta in *The Trial of Witchcraft* (1616) refers to an Italian case in which a woman who had rubbed flying ointment on her body fell into a trance from which she could not be roused. When she finally came around of her own accord, she declared that she had been flying over seas and mountains, and could not be convinced otherwise even though others had witnessed her body lying in an entranced state. Commentators over the years remained divided over whether the witches actually flew or only flew mentally, but [philosopher] Francis Bacon had the measure of the matter in 1608 when he wrote in *Sylva Sylvarum* "I suppose that the soporiferous medicines [in the ointments] are likest to do it."

Flying Ointments

Interestingly, there is little evidence in the confessions of witches that they used flying ointments. Duerr points out that it was in the interest of the Church to downplay the hallucinogenic nature of the flying ointments. If their role was recognized, then the "Devil would then have been left with only a very modest significance, or none at all." But there *are* some records. A Belgian witch called Claire Goessen confessed in 1603 that she had flown to sabbats several times on a staff smeared with an unguent. In northern France in 1460, five women confessed to receiving a salve from the devil himself, which they rubbed on their hands and on a small wooden rod they placed between their legs and flew upon "above good towns and woods and waters." Swedish witches in 1669 rode "over churches and high walls" on a beast given to them by the devil, who also gave them a horn containing a salve with which they anointed themselves. Members of Somerset covens admitted to smearing their foreheads and wrists with a greenish ointment "which smells raw" before their meetings. It may well have been that under the hysteria of the times and the intimidation of the Church authorities, some of those who confessed falsely admitted to the use of ointment—as they clearly bowed to the pressure to say that the ointments were obtained from the devil. But even if this were the case, the idea of ointments itself was a reference to traditional practices that were still known among the rural classes at the time, and that had probably been around for untold generations.

It is known that some of these ointments were actual because certain European writers of the sixteenth and seventeenth centuries recorded recipes for them. Along with animal fat, the blood of bats or lapwings, toads, and other weird and disgusting ingredients, the most commonly listed plants were aconite, hemlock, deadly nightshade, henbane, poppy, and mandrake. . . . Henbane . . . [creates] the sensation of the body feeling light followed by the sensation of flying. Both aconite (*Aconitum* spp.) and hemlock (*Conium maculatum*) were sacred to Hecate, goddess of the earth and the underworld, and both are very poisonous. In German tradition, hemlock (*Conium* means "stimulating dizziness") was home to a toad, which lived beneath it and sucked up its poisons. (Certain toads do have hallucinogenic chemicals in or on their bodies and this might explain their association with witches' brews.) Both plants in nonlethal doses can elicit feelings of flying. Mandrake (*Mandragora officinarum*) owes its enormous importance in magical lore, in part, to the fact that its roots can sometimes look like a human figure, and there were specific folk traditions surrounding its gathering and uprooting. But it also is psychoactive.

Deadly nightshade or belladonna (*Atropa belladonna*) is the classic witchcraft plant. It was known in Old English as *dwayberry*, which derives from the Danish *dvaleboer*, meaning "trance berry," confirming the knowledge of its poisonous and hallucinogenic effects. Belladonna, mandrake, and henbane are members of the *Solanaceae* or nightshade family, as are species of *Datura*, which are or were widely used for ritual hallucinogenic purposes in the Americas and elsewhere. (In fact, thorn apple—*Datura stramonium*, *Datura* spp.—was introduced into Europe from the New World in time to establish itself and become included in witches' brews.) They contain tropane alkaloids, especially hyoscyamine, "a powerful hallucinogen, which gives the sensation of flying through the air . . . among other effects." Michael Harner has observed that atropine is absorbable even through intact skin, so the act of rubbing ointments made from atropine-containing solanaceous plants would be an extremely effective way to become intoxicated. This has been confirmed in recent—and clearly dangerous—experiments. Folklorist Dr. Will-Erich Peuckert of Göttingen, for example, mixed an ointment made up of belladonna, henbane, and datura from a seventeenth-century formula and rubbed it on his forehead and armpits. A number of colleagues did the same. They all fell into a twenty-four-hour sleep. "We had wild dreams. Faces danced before my eyes which were at first terrible. Then I suddenly had the sensation of flying for miles through the air. The flight was repeatedly interrupted by great falls. Finally, in the last phase, an image of an orgiastic feast with grotesque sensual excess," Peuckert reported. [Anthropologist Michael] Harner emphasizes the importance of the greased broomstick or similar flying implement, which he suggests served as "an applicator for the atropine-containing plant to the sensitive vaginal membranes as well as providing the suggestion of riding on a steed, a typical illusion of the witches' ride to the Sabbat."

Animal Transformation

"A characteristic feature of solanaceae psychosis is furthermore that the intoxicated person imagines himself to have been changed into some animal, and the hallucinosis is completed by the sensation of the growing of feathers and hair, due probably to main paraethesic," Erich Hesse claimed in 1946. In 1658, Giovanni Battista Porta wrote that a potion made from henbane, mandrake, thorn apple, and belladonna would make a person "believe he was changed into a Bird or Beast." He might "believe himself turned into a Goose, and would eat Grass, and beat the Ground with his Teeth, like a Goose: now and then sing, and endeavor to clap his Wings." Animal transformation is a primary aspect of the hallucinogenic experience, whether it is a shaman in the Amazon turning into a jaguar, or a Western subject in a psychological experiment. Take this example of the latter, from a series of studies of the effect of harmaline, conducted by psychologist Claudio Naranjo in the 1960s. The subject had felt like a huge bird, then a fish, but then:

> I wasn't a fish anymore, but a big cat, a tiger. I walked, though, feeling the same freedom I had experienced as a bird and a fish, freedom of movement, flexibility, grace. I moved as a tiger in the jungle, joyously, feeling the ground under my feet, feeling my power; my chest grew larger. I then approached an animal, any animal. I only saw its neck, and then experienced what a tiger feels when looking at its prey.

The night travelers and "witches" often thought of themselves as flying animals—owls, farmyard beasts, and, quite often, wolves. Harner has commented that perhaps the ancient and widespread European belief concerning humans turning into wolves—lycanthropy—resulted from hallucinogenic experience, and suggests that the inclusion of animal fat, blood, and body parts in witches' ointments may have been for the purposes of creating the suggestion of becoming an animal.

We can see from this wide-ranging survey that the psychedelic experience was deeply insinuated into the beliefs and practices of the Old World, at least in its ritual and magical aspects—and to a limited extent, in its religious life too. Just how extensive this influence was in the development of Western culture awaits further investigative scholarship, which in turn relies in good measure on the willingness of modern Europeans to be prepared to accept that the emergence of their culture was accompanied by the sort of ceremonial drug practices still surviving in traditional societies such as those to be found in the Americas.

The Native American Peyote Religion

Richard Evans Schultes

In this selection, renowned ethnobotanist Richard Evans Schultes discusses the ritualized use of peyote, a hallucinogenic cactus, among native cultures of North America. For hundreds of years before the arrival of Europeans to the Americas, indigenous tribes ingested peyote for medicinal and religious purposes. Despite strong opposition from some Christian missionaries, the peyote cult spread from Mexico northward into the United States, where it eventually gained legal status after its absorption into the Native American Church. Followers of the peyote religion consider the cactus to be the incarnation of a deity, Schultes explains. For believers, peyote grants access to visions, supernatural spirits, and divine healing.

Since the Cactus family offers some of the most bizarre shapes and forms that evolution has produced in the plant kingdom, it is perhaps understandable that some of the species have become closely connected with native beliefs and ritual practices. But this interesting family contains in the tissues of a number of its species unusual psychoactive constituents even more attractive than outer form to medicinal, religious, and magical aspects of native culture. Undoubtedly the most important of these species is *Lophophora Williamsii*, the peyote cactus.

[In 1651] peyote was first fully described by [the Spanish explorer Francisco] Hernández who called it *Peyotl zacatecensis:*

The root is nearly medium size, sending forth no branches or leaves above the ground, but with a certain woolliness adhering to it on account of which it could not be aptly figured by me. . . . It appears to have a sweetish and moderately hot taste. Ground up and applied to painful joints, it is said to give relief. . . . This root . . . causes those devouring it to foresee and predict things . . . or to discern who has stolen from them some utensil or anything else; and other things of like nature. . . . On which account, this root scarcely issues forth, as if it did not wish to harm those who discover it and eat it.

[Fray Bernardino de] Sahagún, the first European to discuss peyote seriously, suggested that the Toltecas and Chichimecas had employed it for many hundreds of years and that it was a "common food of the Chichimecas," who used it to give them courage to fight and enable them to transcend thirst, hunger, and fear; it was thought to protect them from all danger, and those who ingested it saw "visions either frightful or laughable."

Saint or Diabolical Plant?

In spite of the virulence of early Spanish attempts to stamp out the pagan religion in which peyote figured so prominently, the sacred cactus ritual survived in more or less pure form in the more remote deserts and mountains, while elsewhere it came to be intertwined with Christian ritual and belief. So strongly entrenched in aboriginal thought was this sacred cactus that even certain Christianized Indians of Mexico held that a patron saint—El Santo Niño de Peyotl—used to appear among the plants on the hillsides, a belief that still survives in Mexican folklore. As early as 1591 a chronicler denounced peyote as "satanic trickery." All through the seventeenth century and into the eighteenth, ecclesiastical opposition raged furiously. An eighteenth-century description referred to the cactus as the "diabolic root." In 1720, peyote was prohibited throughout Mexico, and all Indians within reach of the law and church were forced to practice their rituals in secret. The ecclesiastics went so far as to incorporate in a religious manual of 1760 questions in the form of a catechism that equated the eating of peyote with cannibalism! Today the use of peyote by the Huichol, Cora, Tarahumara, and other Indians in their religious ceremonies is no longer illegal; indeed, peyote is freely available in Mexican herb markets as a valued medicinal plant.

The earliest undoubted record of the use of peyote in what is now the territory of the United States dates from 1760 in Texas. The cactus was certainly known to American Indians during the Civil War, but it did not come strongly to public attention until about 1880, when the Kiowa and Comanche tribes began actively to practice and spread a new kind of peyote ceremony, quite different from the peyote rituals of the tribes of northwestern Mexico.

The Spread of the Peyote Cult

The exact route of the introduction of the peyote religion from Mexico into the United States is not known, and there may have been several routes at different periods. Raids into the Mescalero country may have been the principal method of acquainting Plains Indians with the plant and its cult. Slow and gradual diffusion northward almost certainly took place as well. At any rate, the cult was well established among the Kiowas and Comanches between 1880 and 1885 and was being spread with missionary zeal. By the late 1920's, the cult had been forced, by the strong hostility and outright untruthful propaganda of many organized Christian missionary groups, to incorporate itself into the Native American Church—a legally constituted religious sect due the protection and respect enjoyed by any other religious group. In 1920 there were some 13,300 adherents in about thirty tribes. At present [1972], an estimated 250,000 Indians in tribes as far north as Saskatchewan, Canada, practice this religion, which advocates brotherly love, high moral principle, abstention from alcohol, and other admirable teachings.

There is still disagreement about the reasons peyote use

spread so fast, edging out other well-established Indian "na-tivistic" movements, such as the famous Ghost Dance.[1] Ac-cording to [James] Slotkin, an anthropologist who himself be-came an adherent of the peyote church,

> The Peyote Religion was nativistic but not militant. Culturally, it permitted the Indians to achieve a cultural organization in which they took pride. Socially, it provided a supernatural means of accommodation to the existing domination-subordination relation. . . . The Peyote Religion's program of accommodation, as opposed to the Ghost Dance's program of opposition, was the basic reason for the former's success and the latter's failure.

The fact that it could induce visual hallucinations undoubtedly contributed to the rapid spread of peyote through the culture of the Plains region.[2] However, the awe and respect in which the Indians of Mexico and the United States have long held this cactus as supernatural medicine and stimulant—quite apart from its vision-inducing qualities—have probably not been sufficiently appreciated.

Medicinal Power

The tribes of northern Mexico have long ascribed divine origin to peyote. According to the Tarahumara, when Father Sun de-parted from earth to dwell on high, he left peyote behind to cure all man's ills and woes. Its medicinal powers were so

---

1. The Ghost Dance religion, which first arose in 1870 among the Indians of the West-ern Plains, and which ended in 1890 in the tragic massacre of 300 unarmed Sioux at Wounded Knee Creek, was based on the vision . . . that a great mass of mud and wa-ter would soon roll over the earth, destroying the white men and all their gear. The In-dians should dance the old round dance and, as they danced, the flood would roll over them. When it was over, the earth would be green again, animals and plants would be as in the old days, and the ancestral dead would come back.   2. Among North American Indians, especially hunting and gathering tribes, not only shamans but also ordinary men had the capacity to experience visions and obtain the aid of supernat-ural spirits. This could be achieved only through a strenuous "vision quest," involving fasting, thirsting, purification, exposure—even self-mutilation and torture. The result would be a trance or a vivid dream in which the visionary made contact with his fu-ture guardian spirit and perhaps even received some visible token to prove the fact.

great—and its psychoactive effects, of course, are to the Indians the epitome of "medicinal power"—that it was considered a vegetal incarnation of a deity. The legends of its effectiveness as a supernatural medicine have kept peyote from being used hedonistically as a narcotic and have helped to maintain its exalted role as a near-divinity—a place it holds to this day, even among highly acculturated Indian groups in the United States.

In the United States, the Kiowa-Comanche peyote ceremony established during the [nineteenth] century is still followed today, with minor alterations. It usually consists of an all-night meeting with the worshipers sitting in a circle around a peyote altar, led in prayer, chants, and meditation by a "road man." The meeting ends in the morning with a communal meal. This contrasts strongly with the ancient ritual still practiced in northern Mexico, usually a longer ceremony of which dancing is a major part.

North of Mexico, it is usually the dried, discoidal top or crown of the cactus—the "mescal button"—that is chewed and swallowed during the ceremony. In Mexico, the plants are still more or less ceremonially collected where they grow. In many parts of the United States, the Indian peyotists have to purchase the buttons, which, since they are well-nigh indestructible, can be shipped long distances and stored indefinitely.

Lophophora Williamsii represents a veritable factory of alkaloids. More than thirty alkaloids and their amine derivatives—many of them, to be sure, in minute concentrations—have been isolated from the plant. Although most, if not all, of them are in some way or other biodynamically active, their effects are not well understood. They belong mainly to the phenylethylamine and biogenetically related simple isoquinolines. The phenylethylamine mescaline is the vision-inducing alkaloid, and experimental psychology has found mescaline to be of extreme interest as a tool. Other alkaloids are undoubtedly responsible for the tactile, auditory, and occasionally other hallucinations of the peyote intoxication.

Peyote Intoxication

Peyote intoxication, among the most complex and variable effects of all hallucinogenic plants, is characterized by brilliantly colored visions in kaleidoscopic movement, often accompanied by auditory, gustatory, olfactory, and tactile hallucinations. Sensations of weightlessness, macroscopia, depersonalization, and alteration or loss of time perception are normally experienced.

There are very real differences between peyote intoxication and mescaline intoxication. Among aboriginal users, it is the fresh or dried head of the cactus, with its total alkaloid content, that is ingested; mescaline is ingested only experimentally and then produces the effects of but one of the alkaloids, without the physiological interaction of the others that are present in the crude plant material. As a consequence, descriptions of the visual hallucinations of mescaline found in such writings as those of Aldous Huxley should not be equated too closely with the visual effects experienced by Indian peyotists.

Doses vary greatly among Indian users, who may ingest anywhere from four mescal buttons to more than thirty. Peyote intoxication characteristically has two phases: a period of contentment and hypersensitivity followed by calm and muscular sluggishness, often accompanied by hypercerebrality and colored visions. Before visual hallucinations appear, usually within three hours after ingestion of the drug, the subject sees flashes of color across the field of vision, the depth and saturation of the colors (which always precede the visions) defying description. There seems to be a sequence frequently followed in the visions: from geometric figures to familiar scenes and faces to unfamiliar scenes and faces and in some cases objects. The literature is rich in detailed descriptions of visual hallucinations from both peyote and mescaline intoxication, and they provide a wealth of data for psychological and psychiatric research.

Although the visual hallucinations are important in native peyote cults, peyote, as we have said, is revered in large part because of its usefulness as a "medicine." Its medicinal powers, in turn, derive from its ability, through the visions, to put a man into contact with the spirit world, from which, according to aboriginal belief, come illness and even death, and to which the medicine men turn for their diagnoses.

Other Mescaline-Containing Plants

The magico-therapeutic powers of *Lophophora Williamsii* have such wide repute in Mexico that many plants have been confused with or related to it by vernacular terms. They are not all in the cactus family, although a number of cactus species in seven genera, popularly classed as peyotes, are related to *Lophophora* in folklore and folk medicine: *Ariocarpus, Astrophytum, Aztekium, Dolichothele, Obregonia, Pelecyphora,* and *Solisia.* They may have similar toxic effects, may superficially resemble *Lophophora,* or may be used together with *Lophophora.* . . .

Certain species of the tall columnar cactus plants of the high and dry Andes in South America are likewise known to contain alkaloids, including, especially, mescaline. It is, therefore, not suprising that Peruvian Indians have discovered the vision-inducing properties of *Trichocereus* and prepare a hallucinogenic drink from *T. Pachanoi,* known locally as *San Pedro,* which mestizo *curanderos,* or curers, administer to their patients or ingest themselves for purposes of diagnosis, divination, and confrontation with the hostile spirits causing the illness. It also enters an intoxicating drink called *cimora,* which is said to contain extracts of another cactus, the tall, columnar *Neoraimonda macrostibas,* as well as *Isotoma longiflora* (Campanulaceae), *Pedilanthus titimoloides* (Euphorbiaceae), and a species of *Datura* (Solanaceae). Several of these admixtures are alkaloidal and may themselves contain hallucinogenic constituents.

CHAPTER TWO

Experiments with Hallucinogens

How LSD Originated

Albert Hofmann

Born in 1906, Swiss chemist Albert Hofmann is the former director of research for the department of natural products at Sandoz Laboratories, a pharmaceutical firm in Basel, Switzerland. While experimenting with medicinal ergot alkaloids in the late 1930s and early 1940s, Hofmann produced the lysergic acid derivative that came to be known as LSD-25. Hofmann later synthesized psilocybin, the active ingredient in hallucinogenic mushrooms. He is also the author of numerous chemical and pharmaceutical research books. In the following excerpt from his book *LSD: My Problem Child*, Hofmann describes how he first synthesized LSD while attempting to create a drug to enhance blood circulation. He discovered LSD's psychoactive properties after unintentionally ingesting some of the drug during the synthesizing process. Further self-experiments revealed to him the alternately pleasant and disturbing effects of this potent hallucinogen.

I could not forget the relatively uninteresting LSD-25.[1] A peculiar presentiment—the feeling that this substance could possess properties other than those established in the first investigations—induced me, five years after the first synthesis, to produce LSD-25 once again so that a sample could be given to the pharmacological department for further tests. This was

1. Hofmann had first synthesized LSD-25 in 1938 during an investigation of potential circulatory stimulants. Testing of the drug was abandoned because pharmacologists showed little interest in it.

quite unusual; experimental substances, as a rule, were definitely stricken from the research program if once found to be lacking in pharmacological interest.

Nevertheless, in the spring of 1943, I repeated the synthesis of LSD-25. As in the first synthesis, this involved the production of only a few centigrams of the compound.

In the final step of the synthesis, during the purification and crystallization of lysergic acid diethylamide in the form of a tartrate (tartaric acid salt), I was interrupted in my work by unusual sensations. The following description of this incident comes from the report that I sent at the time to Professor Stoll:[2]

> Last Friday, April 16, 1943, I was forced to interrupt my work in the laboratory in the middle of the afternoon and proceed home, being affected by a remarkable restlessness, combined with a slight dizziness. At home I lay down and sank into a not unpleasant intoxicated-like condition, characterized by an extremely stimulated imagination. In a dreamlike state, with eyes closed (I found the daylight to be unpleasantly glaring), I perceived an uninterrupted stream of fantastic pictures, extraordinary shapes with intense, kaleidoscopic play of colors. After some two hours this condition faded away.

This was, altogether, a remarkable experience—both in its sudden onset and its extraordinary course. It seemed to have resulted from some external toxic influence; I surmised a connection with the substance I had been working with at the time, lysergic acid diethylamide tartrate. But this led to another question: how had I managed to absorb this material? Because of the known toxicity of ergot substances, I always maintained meticulously neat work habits. Possibly a bit of the LSD solution had contacted my fingertips during crystallization, and a trace of the substance was absorbed through the skin. If LSD-25 had indeed been the cause of this bizarre experience, then it must be a substance of extraordinary potency. There seemed

---

2. Arthur Stoll was the director of the pharmaceutical department at the Sandoz company.

to be only one way of getting to the bottom of this. I decided on a self-experiment.

Exercising extreme caution, I began the planned series of experiments with the smallest quantity that could be expected to produce some effect, considering the activity of the ergot alkaloids known at the time: namely, 0.25 mg (mg = milligram = one thousandth of a gram) of lysergic acid diethylamide tartrate. Quoted below is the entry for this experiment in my laboratory journal of April 19, 1943.

Self-Experiments

> 4/19/43 16:20: 0.5 cc of ½ promil aqueous solution of diethylamide tartrate orally = 0.25 mg tartrate. Taken diluted with about 10 cc water. Tasteless.
>
> 17:00: Beginning dizziness, feeling of anxiety, visual distortions, symptoms of paralysis, desire to laugh.
>
> Supplement of 4/21: Home by bicycle. From 18:00–ca. 20:00 most severe crisis. . . .

Here the notes in my laboratory journal cease. I was able to write the last words only with great effort. By now it was already clear to me that LSD had been the cause of the remarkable experience of the previous Friday, for the altered perceptions were of the same type as before, only much more intense. I had to struggle to speak intelligibly. I asked my laboratory assistant, who was informed of the self-experiment, to escort me home. We went by bicycle, no automobile being available because of wartime restrictions on their use. On the way home, my condition began to assume threatening forms. Everything in my field of vision wavered and was distorted as if seen in a curved mirror. I also had the sensation of being unable to move from the spot. Nevertheless, my assistant later told me that we had traveled very rapidly. Finally, we arrived at home safe and sound, and I was just barely capable of asking my companion to summon our family doctor and request milk from the neighbors.

In spite of my delirious, bewildered condition, I had brief periods of clear and effective thinking—and chose milk as a nonspecific antidote for poisoning.

The dizziness and sensation of fainting became so strong at times that I could no longer hold myself erect, and had to lie down on a sofa. My surroundings had now transformed themselves in more terrifying ways. Everything in the room spun around, and the familiar objects and pieces of furniture assumed grotesque, threatening forms. They were in continuous motion, animated, as if driven by an inner restlessness. The lady next door, whom I scarcely recognized, brought me milk—in the course of the evening I drank more than two liters. She was no longer Mrs. R., but rather a malevolent, insidious witch with a colored mask.

Even worse than these demonic transformations of the outer world, were the alterations that I perceived in myself, in my inner being. Every exertion of my will, every attempt to put an end to the disintegration of the outer world and the dissolution of my ego, seemed to be wasted effort. A demon had invaded me, had taken possession of my body, mind, and soul. I jumped up and screamed, trying to free myself from him, but then sank down again and lay helpless on the sofa. The substance, with which I had wanted to experiment, had vanquished me. It was the demon that scornfully triumphed over my will. I was seized by the dreadful fear of going insane. I was taken to another world, another place, another time. My body seemed to be without sensation, lifeless, strange. Was I dying? Was this the transition? At times I believed myself to be outside my body, and then perceived clearly, as an outside observer, the complete tragedy of my situation. I had not even taken leave of my family (my wife, with our three children had traveled that day to visit her parents, in Lucerne). Would they ever understand that I had not experimented thoughtlessly, irresponsibly, but rather with the utmost caution, and that such a result was in no way foreseeable? My fear and despair intensified, not only because a young family should lose its father, but also because I dreaded leaving my chemical research work, which meant so much to me, unfinished in the midst of fruitful, promising development. Another reflection took shape, an idea full of bitter irony: if I was now forced to leave this world prematurely, it was because of this lysergic acid diethylamide that I myself had brought forth into the world.

By the time the doctor arrived, the climax of my despondent condition had already passed. My laboratory assistant informed him about my self-experiment, as I myself was not yet able to formulate a coherent sentence. He shook his head in perplexity, after my attempts to describe the mortal danger that threatened my body. He could detect no abnormal symptoms other than extremely dilated pupils. Pulse, blood pressure, breathing were all normal. He saw no reason to prescribe any medication. Instead he conveyed me to my bed and stood watch over me. Slowly I came back from a weird, unfamiliar world to reassuring everyday reality. The horror softened and gave way to a feeling of good fortune and gratitude, the more normal perceptions and thoughts returned, and I became more confident that the danger of insanity was conclusively past.

Now, little by little I could begin to enjoy the unprecedented colors and plays of shapes that persisted behind my closed eyes. Kaleidoscopic, fantastic images surged in on me, alternating, variegated, opening and then closing themselves in circles and spirals, exploding in colored fountains, rearranging and hybridizing themselves in constant flux. It was particularly remarkable how every acoustic perception, such as the sound of a door handle or a passing automobile, became transformed into optical perceptions. Every sound generated a vividly changing image, with its own consistent form and color.

Late in the evening my wife returned from Lucerne. Someone had informed her by telephone that I was suffering a mysterious breakdown. She had returned home at once, leaving the children behind with her parents. By now, I had recovered myself sufficiently to tell her what had happened.

Exhausted, I then slept, to awake next morning refreshed,

with a clear head, though still somewhat tired physically. A sensation of well-being and renewed life flowed through me. Breakfast tasted delicious and gave me extraordinary pleasure. When I later walked out into the garden, in which the sun shone now after a spring rain, everything glistened and sparkled in a fresh light. The world was as if newly created. All my senses vibrated in a condition of highest sensitivity, which persisted for the entire day.

This self-experiment showed that LSD-25 behaved as a psychoactive substance with extraordinary properties and potency. There was to my knowledge no other known substance that evoked such profound psychic effects in such extremely low doses, that caused such dramatic changes in human consciousness and our experience of the inner and outer world.

What seemed even more significant was that I could remember the experience of LSD inebriation in every detail. This could only mean that the conscious recording function was not interrupted, even in the climax of the LSD experience, despite the profound breakdown of the normal world view. For the entire duration of the experiment, I had even been aware of participating in an experiment, but despite this recognition of my condition, I could not, with every exertion of my will, shake off the LSD world. Everything was experienced as completely real, as alarming reality; alarming, because the picture of the other, familiar everyday reality was still fully preserved in the memory for comparison.

Another surprising aspect of LSD was its ability to produce such a far-reaching, powerful state of inebriation without leaving a hangover. Quite the contrary, on the day after the LSD experiment I felt myself to be, as already described, in excellent physical and mental condition.

I was aware that LSD, a new active compound with such properties, would have to be of use in pharmacology, in neurology, and especially in psychiatry, and that it would attract the interest of concerned specialists. But at that time I had no inkling that the new substance would also come to be used beyond medical science, as an inebriant in the drug scene. Since my self-experiment had revealed LSD in its terrifying, demonic aspect, the last thing I could have expected was that this substance could ever find application as anything approaching a pleasure drug. I failed, moreover, to recognize the meaningful connection between LSD inebriation and spontaneous visionary experience until much later, after further experiments, which were carried out with far lower doses and under different conditions.

The next day I wrote to Professor Stoll the above-mentioned report about my extraordinary experience with LSD-25 and sent a copy to the director of the pharmacological department, Professor Rothlin.

As expected, the first reaction was incredulous astonishment. Instantly a telephone call came from the management; Professor Stoll asked: "Are you certain you made no mistake in the weighing? Is the stated dose really correct?" Professor Rothlin also called, asking the same question. I was certain of this point, for I had executed the weighing and dosage with my own hands. Yet their doubts were justified to some extent, for until then no known substance had displayed even the slightest psychic effect in fraction-of-a-milligram doses. An active compound of such potency seemed almost unbelievable.

Professor Rothlin himself and two of his colleagues were the first to repeat my experiment, with only one-third of the dose I had utilized. But even at that level, the effects were still extremely impressive, and quite fantastic. All doubts about the statements in my report were eliminated.

The CIA
Experimentation
with LSD

Martin A. Lee and Bruce Schlain

From the late 1940s through the 1960s, the U.S. Central Intel-ligence Agency (CIA) directed several research programs in-volving mind control, espionage, and weapons development. Responding to the threat posed by the Soviet Union's emer-gence as a world power, CIA operatives conducted experiments with LSD, hoping to develop the drug as a tool for espionage and covert operations. According to researchers Martin A. Lee and Bruce Schlain, these experiments included sneaking LSD into the drinks of CIA personnel and unwitting civilians. Lee and Schlain are the authors of *Acid Dreams: The Complete Social History of LSD*, from which this selection is excerpted.

In a speech before the National Alumni Conference at Princeton University on April 10, 1953, newly appointed CIA director Allen Dulles lectured his audience on "how sinister the battle for men's minds had become in Soviet hands." The human mind, Dulles warned, was a "malleable tool," and the Red Menace [Communists] had secretly developed "brain perversion tech-niques." Some of these methods were "so subtle and so abhor-rent to our way of life that we have recoiled from facing up to them." Dulles continued, "The minds of selected individuals who are subjected to such treatment . . . are deprived of the

Martin A. Lee and Bruce Schlain, *Acid Dreams: The Complete Social History of LSD: The CIA, the Sixties, and Beyond*. New York: Grove Weidenfeld, 1985. Copyright © 1985 by Martin A. Lee and Bruce Schlain. Reproduced by permission of Grove/Atlantic, Inc.; in the UK by permission of Elaine Markson Literary Agency.

ability to state their own thoughts. Parrot-like, the individuals so conditioned can merely repeat the thoughts which have been implanted in their minds by suggestion from outside. In effect the brain . . . becomes a phonograph playing a disc put on its spindle by an outside genius over which it has no control."

Three days after delivering this address Dulles authorized Operation MK-ULTRA, the CIA's major drug and mind control program during the Cold War. MK-ULTRA was the brainchild of Richard Helms, a high-ranking member of the Clandestine Services (otherwise known as the "dirty tricks department") who championed such methods throughout his career as an intelligence officer. As Helms explained to Dulles when he first proposed the MK-ULTRA project, "Aside from the offensive potential, the development of a comprehensive capability in this field . . . gives us a thorough knowledge of the enemy's theoretical potential, thus enabling us to defend ourselves against a foe who might not be as restrained in the use of these techniques as we are."

Intra-Agency Conflicts

The supersecret MK-ULTRA program was run by a relatively small unit within the CIA known as the Technical Services Staff (TSS). Originally established as a supplementary funding mechanism to the ARTICHOKE project,[1] MK-ULTRA quickly grew into a mammoth undertaking that outflanked earlier mind control initiatives. For a while both the TSS and the Office of Security (which directed the ARTICHOKE project) were engaged in parallel LSD tests, and a heated rivalry developed between the two groups. Security officials were miffed because they had gotten into acid first and then this new clique started cutting in on what the ARTICHOKE crowd considered their rightful turf.

The internecine conflict grew to the point where the Office

---

1. ARTICHOKE was the code name for the CIA's research program on mind control, conducted in the 1950s.

of Security decided to have one of its people spy on the TSS. This set off a flurry of memos between the Security informant and his superiors, who were dismayed when they learned that Dr. Sidney Gottlieb, the chemist who directed the MK-ULTRA program, had approved a plan to give acid to unwitting American citizens. The Office of Security had never attempted such a reckless gesture—although it had its own idiosyncrasies; ARTICHOKE operatives, for example, were attempting to have a hypnotized subject kill someone while in a trance.

Whereas the Office of Security utilized LSD as an interrogation weapon, Dr. Gottlieb had other ideas about what to do with the drug. Because the effects of LSD were temporary (in contrast to the fatal nerve agents), Gottlieb saw important strategic advantages for its use in covert operations. For instance, a surreptitious dose of LSD might disrupt a person's thought process and cause him to act strangely or foolishly in public. A CIA document notes that administering LSD "to high officials would be a relatively simple matter and could have a significant effect at key meetings, speeches, etc." But Gottlieb realized there was a considerable difference between testing LSD in a laboratory and using the drug in clandestine operations. In an effort to bridge the gap, he and his TSS colleagues initiated a series of in-house experiments designed to find out what would happen if LSD was given to someone in a "normal" life setting without advance warning.

Experimentation Among Colleagues

They approached the problem systematically, taking one step at a time, until they reached a point where outsiders were zapped with no explanation whatsoever. First everyone in Technical Services tried LSD. They tripped alone and in groups. A typical experiment involved two people pairing off in a closed room where they observed each other for hours at a time, took notes, and analyzed their experiences. As Gottlieb later explained, "There was an extensive amount of self-experimentation for the reason that we felt that a first hand knowledge of the subjective effects of these drugs [was] important to those of us who were involved in the program."

When they finally learned the hallucinogenic ropes, so to speak, they agreed among themselves to slip LSD into each other's drinks. The target never knew when his turn would come, but as soon as the drug was ingested a TSS colleague would tell him so he could make the necessary preparations—which usually meant taking the rest of the day off. Initially the leaders of MK-ULTRA restricted the surprise acid tests to TSS members, but when this phase had run its course they started dosing other Agency personnel who had never tripped before. Nearly everyone was fair game, and surprise acid trips became something of an occupational hazard among CIA operatives. Such tests were considered necessary because foreknowledge would prejudice the results of the experiment.

Indeed, things were getting a bit raucous down at headquarters. When Security officials discovered what was going on, they began to have serious doubts about the wisdom of the TSS game plan. Moral reservations were not paramount; it was more a sense that the MK-ULTRA staff had become unhinged by the hallucinogen. The Office of Security felt that the TSS should have exercised better judgment in dealing with such a powerful and dangerous chemical. The straw that broke the camel's back came when a Security informant got wind of a plan by a few TSS jokers to put LSD in the punch served at the annual CIA Christmas office party. A Security memo dated December 15, 1954, noted that acid could "produce serious insanity for periods of 8 to 18 hours and possibly for longer." The writer of this memo concluded indignantly and unequivocally that he did "not recommend testing in the Christmas punch bowls usually present at the Christmas office parties."

The purpose of these early acid tests was not to explore mystical realms or higher states of consciousness. On the contrary, the TSS was trying to figure out how to employ LSD in espionage operations. Nevertheless, there were times when

CIA agents found themselves propelled into a visionary world and they were deeply moved by the experience. One MK-ULTRA veteran wept in front of his colleagues at the end of his first trip. "I didn't want to leave it," he explained. "I felt I would be going back to a place where I wouldn't be able to hold on to this kind of beauty." His colleagues assumed he was having a bad trip and wrote a report stating that the drug had made him psychotic.

Adverse Reactions

Adverse reactions often occurred when people were given LSD on an impromptu basis. On one occasion a CIA operative discovered he'd been dosed during his morning coffee break. "He sort of knew he had it," a fellow-agent recalled, "but he couldn't pull himself together. Somehow, when you know you've taken it, you start the process of maintaining your composure. But this grabbed him before he was aware, and it got away from him." Then he got away from them and fled across Washington stoned out of his mind while they searched frantically for their missing comrade. "He reported afterwards," the TSS man continued, "that every automobile that came by was a terrible monster with fantastic eyes, out to get him personally. Each time a car passed he would huddle down against a parapet, terribly frightened. It was a real horror for him. I mean, it was hours of agony . . . like being in a dream that never stops—with someone chasing you."

Incidents such as these reaffirmed to the MK-ULTRA crew just how devastating a weapon LSD could be. But this only made them more enthusiastic about the drug. They kept springing it on people in a manner reminiscent of the ritual hazing of fraternity pledges. "It was just too damned informal," a TSS officer later said. "We didn't know much. We were playing around in ignorance. . . . We were just naive about what we were doing."

Such pranks claimed their first victim in November 1953,

when a group of CIA and army technicians gathered for a three-day work retreat at a remote hunting lodge in the backwoods of Maryland. On the second day of the meeting Dr. Gottlieb spiked the after-dinner cocktails with LSD. As the drug began to take effect, Gottlieb told everyone that they had ingested a mind-altering chemical. By that time the group had become boisterous with laughter and unable to carry on a coherent conversation.

One man was not amused by the unexpected turn of events. Dr. Frank Olson, an army scientist who specialized in biological warfare research, had never taken LSD before, and he slid into a deep depression. His mood did not lighten when the conference adjourned. Normally a gregarious family man, Olson returned home quiet and withdrawn. When he went to work after the weekend, he asked his boss to fire him because he had "messed up the experiment" during the retreat. Alarmed by his erratic behavior, Olson's superiors contacted the CIA, which sent him to New York to see Dr. Harold Abramson. A respected physician, Abramson taught at Columbia University and was chief of the allergy clinic at Mount Sinai Hospital. He was also one of the CIA's principal LSD researchers and a part-time consultant to the Army Chemical Corps. While these were impressive credentials, Abramson was not a trained psychiatrist, and it was this kind of counseling his patient desperately needed.

For the next few weeks Olson confided his deepest fears to Abramson. He claimed the CIA was putting something in his coffee to make him stay awake at night. He said people were plotting against him and he heard voices at odd hours commanding him to throw away his wallet—which he did, even though it contained several uncashed checks. Dr. Abramson concluded that Olson was mired in "a psychotic state . . . with delusions of persecution" that had been "crystallized by the LSD experience." Arrangements were made to move him to Chestnut Lodge, a sanitorium in Rockville, Maryland, staffed by CIA-cleared psychiatrists. (Apparently other CIA personnel who suffered from psychiatric disorders were enrolled in this institution.) On his last evening in New York, Olson checked into a room at the Statler Hilton along with a CIA agent assigned to watch him. And then, in the wee hours of the morning, the troubled scientist plunged headlong through a closed window to his death ten floors below.

The Olson suicide had immediate repercussions within the CIA. An elaborate cover-up erased clues to the actual circumstances leading up to his death. Olson's widow was eventually given a government pension, and the full truth of what happened would not be revealed for another twenty years. Meanwhile CIA director Allen Dulles suspended the in-house testing program for a brief period while an internal investigation was conducted. In the end, Gottlieb and his team received only a mildly worded reprimand for exercising "bad judgment," but no records of the incident were kept in their personnel files which would harm their future careers. The importance of LSD eclipsed all other considerations, and the secret acid tests resumed.

Testing Unwitting Targets

Gottlieb was now ready to undertake the final and most daring phase of the MK-ULTRA program: LSD would be given to unwitting targets in real-life situations. But who would actually do the dirty work? While looking through some old OSS [Office of Strategic Services] files, Gottlieb discovered that marijuana had been tested on unsuspecting subjects in an effort to develop a truth serum. These experiments had been organized by George Hunter White, a tough, old-fashioned narcotics officer who ran a training school for American spies during World War II. Perhaps White would be interested in testing drugs for the CIA. As a matter of protocol Gottlieb first approached Harry Anslinger, chief of the Federal Narcotics Bureau. Anslinger was favorably disposed and agreed to "lend" one of his top men to the CIA on a part-time basis.

Right from the start White had plenty of leeway in running

his operations. He rented an apartment in New York's Greenwich Village, and with funds supplied by the CIA he transformed it into a safehouse complete with two-way mirrors, surveillance equipment, and the like. Posing as an artist and a seaman, White lured people back to his pad and slipped them drugs. A clue as to how his subjects fared can be found in White's personal diary, which contains passing references to surprise LSD experiments: "Gloria gets horrors. . . . Janet sky high." The frequency of bad reactions prompted White to coin his own code word for the drug: "Stormy," which was how he referred to LSD throughout his fourteen-year stint as a CIA operative.

Operation Midnight Climax

In 1955 White was transferred to San Francisco, where two more safehouses were established. During this period he initiated Operation Midnight Climax, in which drug-addicted prostitutes were hired to pick up men from local bars and bring them back to a CIA-financed bordello. Unknowing customers were treated to drinks laced with LSD while White sat on a portable toilet behind two-way mirrors, sipping martinis and watching every stoned and kinky moment. As payment for their services the hookers received $100 a night, plus a guarantee from White that he'd intercede on their behalf should they be arrested while plying their trade. In addition to providing data about LSD, Midnight Climax enabled the CIA to learn about the sexual proclivities of those who passed through the safehouses. White's harem of prostitutes became the focal point of an extensive CIA study of how to exploit the art of lovemaking for espionage purposes.

When he wasn't operating a national security whorehouse, White would cruise the streets of San Francisco tracking down drug pushers for the Narcotics Bureau. Sometimes after a tough day on the beat he invited his narc buddies up to one of the safehouses for a little "R & R." Occasionally they unzipped their inhibitions and partied on the premises—much to the chagrin of the neighbors, who began to complain about men with guns in shoulder straps chasing after women in various states of undress. Needless to say, there was always plenty of dope around, and the feds sampled everything from hashish to LSD. "So far as I'm concerned," White later told an associate, "'clear thinking' was non-existent while under the influence of any of these drugs. I did feel at times like I was having a 'mind-expanding experience' but this vanished like a dream immediately after the session."

White had quite a scene going for a while. By day he fought to keep drugs out of circulation, and by night he dispensed them to strangers. Not everyone was cut out for this kind of schizophrenic lifestyle, and White often relied on the bottle to reconcile the two extremes. But there were still moments when his Jekyll-and-Hyde routine got the best of him. One night a friend who had helped install bugging equipment for the CIA stopped by the safehouse only to find the roly-poly narcotics officer slumped in front of a full-length mirror. White had just finished polishing off a half gallon of Gibson's. There he sat, with gun in hand, shooting wax slugs at his own reflection.

Grave Misgivings

The safehouse experiments continued without interruption until 1963, when CIA inspector general John Earman accidentally stumbled across the clandestine testing program during a routine inspection of TSS operations. Only a handful of CIA agents outside Technical Services knew about the testing of LSD on unwitting subjects, and Earman took Richard Helms, the prime instigator of MK-ULTRA, to task for not fully briefing the new CIA director, John J. McCone. Although McCone had been handpicked by President [John] Kennedy to replace Allen Dulles as the dean of American intelligence, Helms apparently had his own ideas about who was running the CIA.

Earman had grave misgivings about MK-ULTRA and he prepared a twenty-four-page report that included a comprehensive overview of the drug and mind control projects. In a cover letter to McCone he noted that the "concepts involved in manipulating human behavior are found by many people within and outside the Agency to be distasteful and unethical." But the harshest criticism was reserved for the safehouse experiments, which, in his words, placed "the rights and interests of U.S. citizens in jeopardy." Earman stated that LSD had been tested on "individuals at all social levels, high and low, native American and foreign." Numerous subjects had become ill, and some required hospitalization for days or weeks at a time. Moreover, the sophomoric procedures employed during the safehouse sessions raised serious questions about the validity of the data provided by White, who was hardly a qualified scientist. As Earman pointed out, the CIA had no way of knowing whether White was fudging the results to suit his own ends.

Earman recommended a freeze on unwitting drug tests until the matter was fully considered at the highest level of the CIA. But Helms, then deputy director for covert operations (the number two position within the Agency), defended the program. In a memo dated November 9, 1964, he warned that the CIA's "positive operational capacity to use drugs is diminishing owing to a lack of realistic testing," and he called for a resumption of the safehouse experiments. While admitting that he had "no answer to the moral issue," Helms argued that such tests were necessary "to keep up with Soviet advances in this field."

Acid Tests in the Military

Rob Evans

In the following essay investigative journalist Rob Evans reveals that the government of the United Kingdom secretly tested LSD on British soldiers in the 1960s. As part of a search for a "humane" chemical weapon, Britain collaborated with Canada and the United States in investigations involving mescaline, LSD, and other drugs, writes Evans. Although LSD proved to be too unpredictable as a weapon, the British and American governments focused on another powerful hallucinogen, BZ, which is easily spread in airborne particles. The author notes that BZ, a long-acting drug that can cause vomiting, blurred vision, confusion, and coma, was packed into thousands of American bombs during the Vietnam War. Evans writes for the British journal the *Guardian;* he is also the author of *Gassed: British Chemical Warfare Experiments on Humans.*

While the police were busting hippies on the streets for dropping LSD during the 1960s, the [British] government's military scientists were administering the same drug to soldiers in secret experiments. Official documents . . . show that the government scientists were also testing acid on animals, mainly rats and cats.

The tests were carried out at the Ministry of Defence's chemical warfare establishment at Porton Down in Wiltshire. Porton Down maintains that the tests were carried out solely to see how soldiers could be protected against LSD if it were

Rob Evans, "Our Lads on LSD," *New Statesman & Society*, vol. 7, October 14, 1994, p. 20.

used by an enemy. But the documents reveal that Porton Down scientists were actively collaborating with American allies in a wide-ranging search for new mind-altering drugs that could be made into an offensive weapon. For three decades, Porton Down has claimed that the public has no reason to worry about what was being done behind its tightly shut doors, but the documents undermine the official line.

Experiments on Animals

Since the first world war, soldiers have been sent to Porton Down to be used as guinea pigs in experiments with chemicals such as nerve gases, mustard gas and tear gas. Porton Down, set up in 1916, is the world's oldest chemical warfare establishment and has enormous expertise and knowledge in this field.

Serious testing of LSD began there in 1960, with a series of experiments on animals. In one test, rats were injected with acid, and it was found, for example, that they detected less often and took longer to run around a maze. In another test, dogs became more restless and introverted, and a cat more timid and clumsy.

In all, experiments on 90 animals were carried out before tests on humans began, but as one document points out, "extrapolation of the results to men is extremely difficult". According to another document, discussions among senior medical officers at the Ministry of Defence produced "slight misgivings in various quarters" over the LSD experiments on troops. Nevertheless, it was agreed that soldiers should undergo psychological tests "to eliminate, if possible, any who may have inherent psychotic tendencies".

Pounds, Shillings, and Pence

Over the next decade, until 1972, 72 soldiers tripped on LSD for the army in three sets of experiments code-named Moneybags, Recount and Small Change. As a sign of Porton's humour, the codenames refer to the coincidence of the letters LSD to pounds, shillings and pence. Porton claims that none of the experiments were underhand, since the soldiers were told beforehand that they were to be tested with LSD. According to Dr Graham Pearson, the current head of Porton, the soldiers were paid an extra 9 pounds on their wages as "compensation for the inconvenience entailed in participating" in each two-week study.

Porton scientists compared the behaviour of soldiers who had been given LSD with those who hadn't. The soldiers were told after the studies which group they had been in. They were monitored to see how they would cope and react, particularly in a military setting. In similar tests in the US, soldiers had to run around an assault course. The British servicemen were given tabs of between 50 and 200 micrograms. An average dose for a fullblown trip of up to 12 hours is 100 to 150 micrograms.

It is not known whether any soldiers suffered bad trips while high in unfamiliar surroundings, nor whether any have had scary flashbacks or are experiencing any distressing mental effects years after the experiments. Porton insists that its tests have never damaged the physical or mental health of any servicemen although, at the same time, the establishment admits that it does not carry out systematic checks that might turn up such damage.

A Humane Weapon?

One of Porton's biggest secrets is its long-standing collaboration with the US in the field of chemical and biological warfare (CBW). Since the second world war, the British and Americans, along with the Canadians and latterly the Australians, have met regularly to discuss and swap freely the results of their CBW efforts. In a network of agreements, the countries set goals and then divided up the tasks to achieve them. The closeness of this relationship is similar to electronic spying, where Britain's GCHQ [Government Communications Headquarters] and its US partner, the National Security Agency, work together very intimately.

In the late 1950s, the Americans became very interested in a new concept in chemical warfare—a "humane" weapon, which, instead of killing people horribly, would merely "incapacitate" them. A public relations campaign was launched in the US to win over the public to the idea of a chemical weapon that would make the enemy giggle and laugh—and give themselves up with their hands behind their backs, without a shot being fired. No doubt, ideally, the enemy would also be whistling the American national anthem.

American scientists started a massive trawl of chemicals to find those that would achieve this effect most efficiently. They were joined in this hunt for so-called "incapacitating agents" by staff at Porton, who investigated mescaline, among other drugs. Official documents from both sides of the Atlantic reveal how Britain and America, along with Canada, teamed up. A Pentagon report shows that, at a conference in 1958, all three countries agreed that they "should concentrate on the search for" incapacitating agents.

The following conference, in 1960, concluded that this was such a "complex problem" that they had to take advantage of the "special capabilities of each country" to "effect the most efficient division of effort in this area". The same conference noted that many of the incapacitating agents "will be solids and may have to be disseminated in sizes that penetrate the respiratory tract" and so "all three countries should consider the dissemination of solid materials as a matter of urgency".

By the next conference, in 1962, the allies were happy to find that: "The varied approaches taken to the search of incapacitating agents in the three countries have contributed to the discovery of significant numbers of (chemicals) of potential interest". An internal Porton paper from that year was entitled "Current investigations in the search for new CW [chemical weapons] agents", noting that "promising leads" were being pursued.

However, these documents are remarkable because, for decades, the British government has insisted that Porton gave up all offensive research to develop new chemical weapons in 1956. This line has been trotted out whenever anyone has questioned what goes on at the establishment. Repeatedly, in answers to recent parliamentary questions from Labour MPs, Porton has insisted that all its work since that year has been devoted to developing defensive equipment and clothing to protect the armed forces. This point is important, because suspicion and mistrust has always dogged efforts to agree to an international treaty to ban chemical weapons from the world.

After years of tortuous negotiations, such a treaty is now in the process of being signed and ratified. One of its provisions requires countries to come clean and declare all its offensive activities in the past. If the Ministry of Defence appears to be lying over what it was doing 30 years ago, what confidence can other countries and the British public have that Porton has not been up to anything naughty in more recent times?

BZ Bombs

After all their efforts, the British and the Americans found that LSD was simply too unpredictable as a weapon. There was no guarantee that the enemy field marshals would capitulate giggling, rather than fire off all their guns and artillery in a fit of paranoia. The Americans had instead settled on another drug—called BZ—which in the mid-1960s was packed into thousands of bombs. They found that, compared to LSD and the other psycho-chemicals they had tested, BZ was potentially easier to use as a weapon since it could be disseminated in an airborne cloud.

According to medical experts, BZ—featured in the film *Jacob's Ladder*—can affect victims for up to four days. It can cause increased heart rate, dry mouth, vomiting, blurred vision and slurred speech, leading to confusion and stupor. Britain conducted its own experiments on BZ between 1960 and 1975, testing it on 25 soldiers and 350 animals, mainly rats and mice. Under the intimate agreements between the two countries, Porton Down—then in theory completely committed to defensive work—shared the fruits of this research with America, then pouring millions of dollars into building a factory to produce BZ bombs.

Aside from these questions over its offensive work, Porton is facing another growing problem. More and more soldiers are casting aside the Official Secrets Act and going public to protest about their role as guinea pigs in the tests involving nerve, mustard and riot gases. They are demanding the truth about the tests on them and, moreover, compensation, since they suspect that their health has been damaged by those experiments.

The Good Friday Experiment of April 1962

Timothy Leary

Researcher and psychology professor Timothy Leary (1920–1996) taught at Harvard University in the early 1960s, where he and colleague Richard Alpert formed the Harvard Psychedelic Drug Research Project to study the effects of hallucinogens on humans. Harvard fired Leary in 1963, but he continued to research hallucinogens, becoming a prominent advocate for the recreational and therapeutic use of LSD. He also came to be seen as a controversial and charismatic rebel as he invited people to "turn on, tune in, and drop out." The following selection is an excerpt from Leary's book *High Priest,* in which the author describes a university-sponsored experiment examining the effects of psilocybin on twenty students who were preparing for religious ministry. This experiment was a component of a doctoral dissertation by Walter N. Pahnke, a Protestant minister and resident in psychiatry at Massachusetts Mental Health Center in Boston. Hallucinogens were legally available to researchers in 1962, when this experiment took place, and Leary, Pahnke, and their colleagues wanted to prove that such drugs could induce religious experiences. The group's findings, however, were largely met with disapproval.

That Spring of 1962 was a rock-and-roll religious revival season. My house was swarming with Christian ministers and Hindu practitioners. We spent a lot of time at the Vedanta ashram. Conversions and rebirths occurring on a relentless weekly schedule.

LSD used as a sacrament was working. . . . And so was Walter Pahnke working. He was doggedly going ahead with plans for his controlled experiment. I had gone along with Walter all along, humoring him, knowing that it couldn't happen. But Walter Pahnke was unstoppable. A master politician in the art of the feasible.

First he cooled me out. He agreed to change his design. There would be no turning-on of a large group, no marching around of masses of people stoned out of their minds. Walter agreed to divide the sample into five small groups. In each group there would be four divinity students—two of whom would be given psilocybin (the sacred mushroom in pill form) and the other two a placebo (a non-psychedelic pill). Each group would be guided by two members of our Harvard project—psychedelic veterans—one of whom would take psilocybin and one of whom would get the placebo.

No one, not even Walter Pahnke, would know who would get the sacrament and who would draw the inactive pill.

No Doctor-Patient Games

Walter balked at the guides taking the drug. This was the main objection which psychiatrists and self-appointed researchers were leveling at our work. How can doctors take drugs with the subjects? The psychiatrists and scientists who were denouncing our work had never taken a psychedelic. To them LSD and psilocybin made you drunk like booze or crazy like mental hospitals. In their Torquemada fantasies we were reeling around intoxicated (or worse). How could we be objective?

But I insisted. There can be no doctor-patient game going when you use psychedelics. We are all in it together. Shared ignorance. Shared hopes. Shared risks. One guide (selected by lot) would be straight and one would be high. And all ten guides would be seeking the same thing as the subjects—a deep spiritual experience on Good Friday.

Walter agreed.

Next, Walter went to the administrators at the three schools and reassured them. The implausible breadth and scope of the experiment was itself an advantage. The fact that three colleges were involved allowed for administrative buck-passing. After all, reasoned Boston University, it's a Harvard doctoral dissertation. After all, reasoned Harvard, our students are not involved as subjects. After all, reasoned Andover-Newton, it's

 THE HISTORY ❧ OF DRUGS

Hallucinogens and Religious Experience

Now, four days after the experience itself, I continue to feel a deep sense of awe and reverence, being simultaneously intoxicated with an ecstatic joy. This euphoric feeling . . . includes elements of profound peace and steadfastness, surging like a spring from a depth of my being which has rarely, if ever, been tapped prior to the drug experience. The spasmodic nature of my prayer life has ceased, and I have yielded to a need to spend time each day in meditation which, though essentially open and wordless, is impregnated by feelings of thanksgiving and trust. . . .

The feelings I experienced could best be described as cosmic tenderness, infinite love, penetrating peace, eternal blessing and unconditional acceptance on one hand, and on the other, an unspeakable awe, overflowing joy, primeval humility, inexpressible gratitude and boundless devotion. Yet all of these words are hopelessly inadequate and can do little more than meekly point towards the genuine, inexpressible feelings actually experienced.

Christian ministerial student, quoted in Walter N. Pahnke, *LSD, Man, and Society*, Richard C. DeBold and Russell C. Leaf, eds., 1969.

really a Harvard-Boston University project. Our students are involved as individuals.

Solid Backing

And then Walter had some powerful sacred cows going for him. He was an M.D., a minister, a Harvard scientist. But more important were the good human energies he had going for him. First there was his own unmistakable sincerity and his reassuring, square, conventional, earnest solidity.

Then he had the backlog of solid spiritual power that had been a-building up over the past year. Every theologian, minister, and administrator in the Boston area had felt the ripple of our religious project. We had provided (in safety) deep, shattering, spiritual conversion experiences for a good two dozen members of the academic establishment. The good word had got around.

Then, and perhaps most important, Walter had the full support of at least one impressive, high-status person at each institution. Professor Huston Smith of M.I.T.—saintly, benevolent, articulate, sound, mature—would be a guide and take the pill blindly on Good Friday and risk going out of his mind.

And Dr. Walter Clark of Andover-Newton—convincing, mellow, lovable—was ready to take the sacrament with strangers and lend his guiding wisdom.

And at Harvard, Walter Pahnke's thesis-adviser was behind the experiment.

So during the Lenten weeks we divided into groups, and the two guides met with the four students and got to know each other and shared concerns and aspirations and ignorances. You see, the groups had this great thing in common. The sharing of goal and risk. No one knew who would receive the sacrament. We were all in it together.

So, much to my amazement, the project came down to the final week with high enthusiasm and competent preparations. The little band of worshipers drew close together, and the ad-

ministrators in the Roman centers of pharisaic power remained nervously silent. By God, and by miracle, it was apparently going to happen. . . .

Good Friday

We assembled at the Seminary at ten [on Friday] morning. The
guides would drive the students to the ceremony. Five rooms in
the basement of the Boston University chapel were reserved for
the groups. My group of six sat around waiting. The students
had Bibles. Pahnke walked in with the envelopes—each coded.
In each envelope was a capsule containing white powder.

I asked one of the students to say a prayer and we remained
in silence for a while and then we took the pill.

Then we all sat waiting to discover what we had taken. The
students were reading their Bibles, but I guessed they weren't
concentrating on the words.

After a while I felt something changing inside. Ah. Good! I
got the psilocybin. I waited. My skin became pink and flushed
with heat. Hello. That's odd. Never felt like this from psilocybin. Soon my body was radiating heat but my consciousness
was unchanged. Then I realized what had happened. Pahnke
had given us a placebo with a somatic kick to fool us. I found
out later it was nicotinic acid.

I looked up and saw that two students had flushed faces.
They were squirming with pleased expressions. One of them
winked at the other. He rose and said he was going to the toilet. The other red-faced student joined him. As guide, I trailed
along. Inside the john they were exulting like happy conspira-
tors. We must have got the mushroom. Yeah, I can feel it. We're
the lucky ones. I smiled and kidded them about playing the
placebo game. While we stood there the door banged open. A
third student from our group walked in. He looked neither left
nor right. No greetings. His eyes were glowing and he was smiling. He walked to the window and stood for a long time looking out. Jesus, he cried, God is everywhere. Oh the Glory of it!

Then he walked out without a word. No social games with him.

The two red-faced students looked solemn. Hopes dashed.

It's a ridiculous ritual to run a double blind study using psychedelic drugs. After thirty minutes everyone knows what has happened, who has taken the sacrament.

In the Chapel

Just before noon Pahnke came through and had us all go to the small chapel. Thirty of us sat in the dim candlelight. Dean Howard Thurmond came in, robed and vested. He spoke a few words. Quietly, serenely. He blessed us and left.

Then through the speakers we could hear him begin his three-hour service in the main chapel above. Prayers. Organ music. Hymns.

It was easy to tell who had taken the psychedelics. Ten students sat attentively like good worshipers. Facing the altar. Silent. The others were less conventional. Some lay on the benches—one lay on the floor. Some wandered around the chapel murmuring in prayer and wonderment. One chanted a hymn. One wandered to the altar and held his hands aloft. One sat at the organ bench and played weird, exciting chords.

The Restless Mystic

One wanted to go out. The doors to the basement were locked and a doorkeeper was on guard. I told Pahnke I'd accompany his restless mystic. We walked along the avenue. Cars whizzed by. I felt fear and moved to the street side of my charge. I had a fantasy he might run out in the avenue. He, of course, read my mind. You are so brutally aware of where things are at during a session. Telepathy?

He glanced at me, as if to say, Is that the game? So he tried to edge by me to walk on the curb. I got more scared. He made a feint to run into the street. My paranoia had forced him into the role of prisoner, seeking to escape.

Then I caught on and laughed. Let's not play that silly game, I said. He nodded. We walked around the chapel. He was out of his mind. Confused. Struggling for meaning. What is it all about? Who is running the show? What am I supposed to do?

We walked back to the basement. My student was still frightened. I kept too close to him. My concern alarmed him. He ran to the piano and banged down the lid savagely. He ran to the wall and grabbed a picture, holding it above his head ready to smash it if he were approached.

I sat down quickly and put my hands in the position of prayer and called him. He stared at me for a long minute. Then he relaxed. About the least threatening thing you can do to another human being is to sit down in the prayer position in front of him. It always works.

He came over and sat down in front of me. I motioned for him to place his hands in prayer. He looked at me in panic and raised his fists. I looked in his eyes—flaming in terror. Is that what hands are for? To destroy . . . to grab . . . to hit . . . oh, you good Christian, have you forgotten your religion? Don't you remember that hands are for worship? For prayer? I grabbed his hands. He started to pull away but held on. He really liked the physical contact and the gentle control. Your hands are for prayer. Let us pray, brother. I held his hands tight and started chanting . . . God . . . Jesus Christ . . . man . . . God . . . Jesus Christ . . . man. . . . His body visibly relaxed. Then he smiled. Then he looked at my face in reverent love. He embraced me. I held him in my arms. About ten people were watching in awed curiosity. I could feel the warmth of his body and the trembling. He began to stroke my hair. His caress became sexual. I took his hands and placed mine around his in the position of prayer. Then I began chanting the Lord's Prayer. Our Father . . . yes, all our Fathers . . . who are in Heaven . . . yes, who art inside Heaven. Inside. I thumped my chest and his. Our Father who art within . . . Hallowed be thy name . . . yes, holy be all thy names . . . Sacred Fathers and

Grandfathers . . . Holy ancestors. . . . Thanks, Holy Father, for living and dying to create us, and give us through seed and sperm our birth to life. . . . Thy Kingdom come. Thy will be done . . . out here on earth, in this room, here in Boston as it is in Heaven within.

He was whispering the words over and over again. Our Father. Holy be thy name. Thy will be done. Then he burst into tears and sobs. He crumbled to the floor. I held him while his body shook with the convulsive heaving.

Then he sat up and looked at me and said, Thanks. I'm all right now. I've been a religious phony and a sexual freak but now I know what prayer is all about.

A Spiritual Test

The afternoon slowly spun itself out. No other scenes of disorder. Much silent meditation. Later hushed talking.

By five o'clock the group was pretty well out of visionary terrain. Pahnke was busy collecting interviews on a tape recorder. He was most conscientious about his data.

The plan was that we would all go to my home for a communion supper. The psychedelic students were in no hurry. They wandered around smiling serenely and looking at flowers. The non-psychedelic students were bored and impatient.

The scene at my house was gentle and radiant. The trippers were still too much in it, still a little high and too stunned to do much except shake their heads in wonder and grin and say, Wow! I never realized. . . .

I was in the kitchen having a celebration beer. Walter Pahnke bustled in. Our eyes met and we grinned and shook hands, laughing.

It was like the first session at the prison. We had done it! We had proved once again that goodwill, and good motives, and trust and courage are the basic research tools. It was a great spiritual test for all of us and we would never forget that Good Friday afternoon of death, fear, ecstasy and rebirth.

Drugs as Sacrament

In the next few weeks the results of the Good Friday session kept feeding back.

Pahnke had teams of interviewers (who knew nothing about the study) collecting the stories of the twenty students, rating the comments and kinds of religious experience.

The results were clear-cut and consistent. The men who ate the mushrooms had mystic religious experiences. The control group didn't.

There was proof—scientific, experimental, statistical, objective. The sacred mushrooms, administered in a religious setting to people who were religiously motivated, did produce that rare, deep experience which men have sought for thousands of years through sacraments, through flagellation, prayer, renunciation.

Psychedelic drugs were sacraments.

To anyone whose values are spiritual, this study had to be the most important research of the last few thousand years. Galileo, Newton, Einstein, Oppenheimer developed theories and methods for understanding and controlling external energies. What produces motion? How can motive power be improved, accelerated? Discoveries of dubious benefit in their application.

But the scientific demonstration that internal energies, ecstasy, revelation, spiritual union, no longer need be accidental but can be produced for and by him who seeks—this can't be underestimated.

You would expect that every priest, minister, rabbi, theologian, philosopher, scholar, or just plain God-seeking man, woman, and child, in the country would drop their secular games and follow up the implications of the Good Friday study.

The Reaction

But you know what happened? The same reaction that has greeted every new spiritual discovery in history. Disapproval. Apathy. Opposition. Why?

The trustees of the Divinity School moved to silence Dr. Walter Clark. But they couldn't. This gentle, thoughtful man consulted his conscience and refused to keep silent. But follow-up studies at the Seminary were stopped, and the divine enthusiasm of the divinity students was blocked and dissipated.

Walter Pahnke got his thesis uneasily approved, and his degree was awarded. Walter went to Germany on a fellowship and arranged to have his first conversation with God in a mental hospital in the Rhineland. He had a clinical examination room converted into a shrine and got a Yale theologian to be his guide, and played sacred music on his record player, and to the shocked amazement of the German psychiatrists (who are using LSD to produce dirty psychoanalytic experiences), Walter made the eternal voyage and laughed in gratitude and wept in reverence. And only then, a year later, did he realize the wondrous miracle he had wrought in Marsh Chapel.

But he wasn't allowed to continue his work. His subsequent requests for government approval to repeat his study have been denied. The last thing the federal Food and Drug Administration seems to want is the production of religious experiences.

Dr. Goddard, the aggressive, hard-driving political medic who runs the F.D.A., derided claims that LSD produces psychological or spiritual benefits. Pure bunk, said Goddard. This from a government official who had never taken or given a psychedelic chemical, nor observed its effects. How can our country's top pharmacological commissar blatantly reject scientific data which doesn't fit his atheistic bias? . . .

A Classic Religious Struggle

The miracle of Marsh Chapel was not just a scientific study; it was authentic spiritual ceremony. And like every valid Good Friday experiment our spring solstice death-rebirth-celebration (because it worked) invited excommunication and persecution. We were involved, not in a controversial research project, but in a classic religious struggle.

The arena for this struggle is always within. The stakes of the game were no longer academic prestige or scientific renown but the souls of the protagonists.

The psychedelic drugs are sacraments, and like all sacraments that work, they demand your all. They demand that you live up to the revelation.

Like all sacraments, the psychedelic drugs threaten society and that part of your own mind that is attached to the current social taboos.

Like all new sacraments, the psychedelics require a new religion.

CHAPTER THREE

Hallucinogens and the Counterculture

Timothy Leary: America's Psychedelic Prophet

Robert C. Fuller

Psychological researcher Timothy Leary played a prominent role in the drug-influenced culture of the 1960s, writes Robert C. Fuller in the following selection. Leary became enthusiastic about hallucinogens after trying psilocybin mushrooms in 1960, and he cofounded a research center at Harvard University to study the effects of various hallucinogens on consciousness. Hundreds of students, clergy, convicts, and artists participated in these investigations, but Leary was fired from Harvard after rumors spread that his research had escalated into wild partying. Leary continued to study and write about the metaphysical aspects of the hallucinogenic experience, and many saw him as a significant influence on the emerging hippie culture as well as the driving force behind the popularity of marijuana and LSD in the 1960s. Leary was jailed on drug charges in 1970, but he escaped from prison and lived in exile overseas until he was caught and returned to the United States three years later. After his parole in the mid-1970s, Leary continued to promote the psychedelic adventure until his death in 1996. Fuller is the author of several books, including *Stairways to Heaven: Drugs in American Religious History*.

The year 1960 turned out to be a critical one in the social history of psychedelics in the United States. Prior to this time, LSD—while legal—was for the most part confined to the laboratories of a handful of pharmaceutical and psychological researchers. Yet larger social forces were at work that were destined to implicate LSD in a major cultural revolution. The transformation of LSD from laboratory alkaloid to cultural icon is a fascinating story in American history. And like most good stories, this one centers around a main character of mythic proportions. In the summer of 1960, Timothy Leary took a vacation to Mexico before beginning his new job at Harvard's Center for the Study of Personality. A Berkeley psychologist, Frank Barron, had told Tim about the psilocybin mushrooms (*teonanacatl*, the "flesh of the gods") that had played such an important role in classic shamanism. Leary, who later described himself as someone who had never met a drug he didn't like, purchased a few of these sacred mushrooms and gave them a try. "The journey lasted a little over four hours," he wrote. "Like almost everyone who had the veil drawn, I came back a changed man."

When Leary assumed his duties that fall at Harvard he found that he had little interest in the relatively boring field of personality assessment. Statistical analyses of questionnaire responses paled by comparison to the wonders unleashed by the psilocybin, mescaline, and LSD he was experimenting with on a nearly daily basis. Leary and his colleague Richard Alpert shifted their research interests in a way that allowed them to turn their favorite hobby into a full-time occupation. Within months they had managed to become the directors of what they christened the Harvard Psychedelic Drug Research Project. During the next four years, Leary and Alpert managed to "arrange transcendent experiences" for over 1,000 persons. Their subjects included students, writers, artists, convicts, and sixty-nine members of the clergy. Also notable for their participation in Leary's investigations were Aldous Huxley, Allen Ginsberg, Alan Watts, and Huston Smith. Although Leary was the most charismatic prophet of the psychedelic gospel, these latter individuals were among the most able apostles.

Psychedelic Spirituality

Leary and Alpert focused principally on studying the ways in which "set" and "setting" influenced the nature of an LSD trip. Their studies indicated that when the setting was supportive but not explicitly spiritual, between 40 and 75 percent of their test subjects nonetheless reported life-changing religious experiences. Yet when the set and setting emphasized spiritual themes, up to 90 percent reported having mystical or illuminating experiences.

Leary was only an advisor and experimental subject in the most famous of these studies on psychedelic spirituality. In the spring of 1962, a graduate student in the Philosophy of Religion program at Harvard Divinity School approached Leary about an exciting project. Walter Pahnke was an M.D. and a minister. He now wanted to earn a degree in religion by conducting an empirical test of the categories scholars use to describe the mystical experience. Pahnke enlisted the help of twenty theology students who gathered on Good Friday at Boston University's Marsh Chapel. The test was a controlled, double-blind experiment in which he divided the twenty subjects into five groups of four students each. Ninety minutes before the Good Friday service began, Pahnke administered identical capsules to each subject. Half of the capsules contained thirty milligrams of psilocybin. The other half contained two hundred milligrams of a vitamin that causes feelings of warmth and tingling but has no effect on the mind. The subjects then attended a two-and-a-half-hour religious service consisting of organ music, prayers, and personal meditation. The subjects were later interviewed and asked to fill out a 147-item questionnaire designed to measure phenomena related to a typology of mystical consciousness. Of note is the fact that nine of the ten students who had taken the psilocybin reported

Timothy Leary encouraged people to seek spiritual enlightenment through the use of psychedelic drugs.

having religious experiences, while only one of the subjects who had been given a placebo reported any such sensations. Pahnke maintained that psychedelics extinguish the "empirical ego" and assist individuals in transcending the subject-object dichotomy of ordinary rational consciousness. His study concluded that LSD occasions every major characteristic of "authentic" mystical experience (e.g., sense of unity, transcendence of space and time, alleged ineffability, paradoxicality, and subsequent elevation of mood). One of Pahnke's group leaders, Walter Clark, surmised that the miracle of Marsh Chapel was "the most cogent single piece of evidence that psychedelic chemicals do, under certain circumstances, release profound religious experience."

Chemical Promiscuity

Leary and Alpert believed that discoveries such as these were about to usher in a new era in human spiritual consciousness.

They believed that they were on the verge of reducing centuries of theological abstractions down to a simple chemical formula. Their studies indicated that if the proper training and setting could be provided, nearly everyone was capable of achieving a sense of mystical oneness with God. Yet much to their surprise and dismay, the world did not run to embrace the implications of their research. Scorn, not praise, met their psychedelic gospel. Part of this disapproval was theological. Already scholars were contending that the "nature mysticism" engendered by LSD was not true or authentic mysticism. However, the central objection to Leary's seemingly indiscriminate advocacy of psychedelics was concern over widespread licentiousness, particularly among youth. The use of LSD was spreading across the country. Easily synthesized in makeshift chemistry labs (and legal until late 1966), the availability of LSD and other psychedelics escalated while the price continued to drop. Chemical euphoria was instantly accessible to the emerging "hippie" culture. Leary frequently warned against misuse and hoped that psychedelics would be restricted to the philosophical elite. But if his words cautioned discretion, his overall demeanor and actions fostered chemical promiscuity. Harvard had made Leary and Alpert pledge not to use undergraduate students in their "research." They never complied. Reports of ribald partying and sexual dalliance in Leary's office swept across campus. Harvard officials had no recourse but to remove both Leary and Alpert from the faculty and shut down their center for psychedelic research.

For a short time, Leary became a rebel without an expense account. His colleague, Richard Alpert, later ventured to India, where he took up the practice of yoga meditation and changed his name to Ram Dass. Alpert had found that the psychedelic experience ultimately led nowhere. Now, in the transformed incarnation of Ram Dass, he continued to believe that psychedelics were of value in helping a person break out of their restricted consciousness. But Ram Dass maintained that such an awakening is only the beginning of an authentic spiritual life.

Thus while never renouncing the possibility that drugs might introduce persons to spiritual dimensions of reality, Alpert shifted the focus of his countercultural ministry to Hindu-style meditation and spiritual discipline.

Leary, however, was more determined than ever to advance the cause of psychedelics. Believing that he could generate sufficient income from his writings, speaking fees and donations, Leary organized the International Federation for Internal Freedom (IFIF) in 1963 for the purpose of continuing his psychedelic research. After being expelled from the organization's original headquarters in Zihuatanejo, Mexico, Leary was offered the use of an estate located in Millbrook, New York. The Millbrook estate provided the perfect setting in which to engage in outlandish behaviors that ranged from serious research to bacchanalian debauchery. For about four years Millbrook was a monastery, school, research laboratory, religious commune, and opium den all rolled into one. The sixty-four-room manor was home not only to the IFIF (subsequently renamed the League for Spiritual Discovery, and finally the Castalia Foundation in reference to the monastery in Hermann Hesse's *The Glass-Bead Game*) but also to a constantly revolving door of visitors who came for drugs, sex, and stimulating conversation. Leary even turned Millbrook into a weekend getaway for those with discretionary income to spend on "consciousness-expanding" retreats. All the while Leary was taking notes on his and others' experiences in an attempt to create a map of the previously unexplored regions of the mind.

Uniting East and West

Leary and others were increasingly persuaded that LSD was giving Westerners access to regions of the mind that practitioners of Eastern meditation systems had known for centuries. For this reason he hoped that Eastern texts might be of great value in his attempt to create a cartography of inner space. Leary first adapted the verses of the *Tao Te Ching* in a book he called *Psychedelic Prayers*. Then, in 1962, he, Ralph Metzner, and Richard Alpert created a psychedelic variation on the Buddhist scholar W.Y. Evans-Wentz's translation of *The Tibetan Book of the Dead*. *The Tibetan Book of the Dead* is an ancient Buddhist meditation manual that purports to explain the realities (termed *bardos*) into which one travels following physical death. It was originally designed to be read to those near death in order to prepare them for the next stage of their metaphysical journey. Leary, Metzner, and Alpert titled their version *The Psychedelic Experience*. They were convinced that the dissolution of the ego afforded by LSD permitted entry into the same realms of consciousness described in Buddhist metaphysics. *The Psychedelic Experience* blended the esoteric terminology of Eastern mystical thought with buzzwords then current in popular American psychology. In this way the Millbrook pundits helped steer their readers to the insight that psychedelic research had at last uncovered the fundamental truths uniting East and West. This volume eventually went through sixteen editions and was translated into seven languages, giving it a long-lasting influence upon subsequent understandings of the realities disclosed by a psychedelic adventure.

Trouble in Paradise

Catastrophes had a way of following Leary. His obvious wit and the constant twinkle in his eyes endeared him to many. But his theatrical excess and cavalier ways frightened others. Drugs were beginning to destroy the lives of a good many young people, and Leary was an obvious target for blame. Leary himself had been arrested in 1965 for possessing marijuana as he attempted to cross the Mexican border. Despite his argument that marijuana had a legitimate religious use and thus the arrest violated his First Amendment rights, he was convicted by a Texas jury. The conviction was eventually overturned, but in the meantime Millbrook was itself raided by G. Gordon Liddy (who was destined to become a symbol and spokesperson for conservative American culture when the Watergate scandal thrust him into national prominence). Liddy, then the assistant district attorney of Dutchess County, led a small troop of law enforcement officials in a midnight raid with the hopes of finding Leary with his pants down and his head turned on. Just what was going on at Millbrook when the police came busting through the doors is still a matter of dispute. Ironically, Liddy and Leary eventually reunited as friends and colleagues on the college lecture circuit and turned their conflicting accounts of the event into entertaining repartee. One thing was clear, however: Government toleration of psychedelics was nearing an end. By 1967 California made the manufacture or possession of LSD illegal. Leary's never-ending attacks upon "the system" were drawing a response. And in 1970, Leary was again convicted of drug possession and sentenced to a minimum security prison in San Luis Obispo. Leary managed to escape from prison and live in exile outside the United States for several years before being caught and returned to prison. Finally released in 1976, Leary continued to promote the psychedelic cause until his death in 1996 (his ashes were sent up in a satellite to orbit earth, which seemed a somewhat apt transition from navigating inner space to orbiting outer space).

Following his 1970 arrest, Leary never quite regained the peculiar role he had achieved in advocating a new, drug-enhanced spirituality. Yet by this time he had already succeeded in spreading his psychedelic gospel throughout the country. The Haight-Ashbury district of San Francisco had surfaced as the Vatican of the Acid Church as early as 1965, giving the psychedelic cause a geographical and symbolic foothold in the terrain of a newly emerging segment of American culture. No one ever quite rivaled Timothy Leary as the High Priest of America's new spiritual consciousness; he and his apostles had spread the psychedelic gospel far and wide.

On the Bus with the Merry Pranksters

Tom Wolfe

The Merry Pranksters were a circle of artists, writers, and musicians who associated with Ken Kesey, author of *One Flew Over the Cuckoo's Nest*, and Neal Cassady, a famous beatnik personality. In the mid-1960s, Kesey, Cassady, and the Pranksters traveled throughout the United States in a bus painted in psychedelic colors they named "Furthur," taking hallucinogens and engaging in street theater and satirical confrontations with authority. The group also hosted "acid tests," festivals at which they would distribute LSD to their guests. One of these acid tests is alleged to have spawned the Grateful Dead, a psychedelic rock band; consequently, the Merry Pranksters are often seen as instigators of and evangelists for the hippie counterculture of the 1960s. The following passage from Tom Wolfe's *The Electric Kool-Aid Acid Test* vividly re-creates the beginning of the Merry Pranksters' crosscountry journey. Wolfe is a journalist and the author of several books, including *The Right Stuff* and *Bonfire of the Vanities*.

On the second day they reached Wikieup, an old Wild West oasis out in the Arizona desert along Route 60. It was all gray-brown desert and sun and this lake, which was like a huge slimy kelp pond, but the air was fantastic. Sandy felt great. Then Kesey held the second briefing. They were going to take their first acid of the trip here and have their first major movie production. He and Babbs and the gorgeous sexy Paula Sundsten were going to take acid—*Wikieup!*—and the others were going to record what happened. Hagen and Walker were going to film it, Sandy was going to handle the sound, and Ron Bevirt was going to take photographs.

Sandy feels his first twinge of—what? Like . . . there is going to be Authorized Acid only. And like . . . they are going to be separated into performers and workers, stars and backstage. Like . . . there is an inner circle and an outer circle. This was illogical, because Hagen and Walker, certainly, were closer to Kesey than any other Pranksters besides Babbs, and they were "workers," too, but that was the way he feels. But he doesn't say anything. Not . . . out front.

Kesey and Babbs and Paula hook down some acid orange juice from the refrigerator and wait for the vibrations. Paula is in a hell of a great mood. She has never taken LSD before, but she looks fearless and immune and ready for all, and she hooks down a good slug of it. They wait for the vibrations . . . and here they come.

Babbs has a big cane, a walking stick, and he is waving it around in the air, and the three of them, Babbs, Kesey and Paula, go running and kicking and screaming toward the lake and she dives in—and comes up with her head covered in muck and great kelpy strands of green pond slime—and beaming in a way that practically radiates out over the face of the lake and the desert. She has surfaced euphoric—

"Oooooh! It sparkles!"

—pulling her long strands of slime-slithering hair outward with her hands and grokking and freaking over it—

"Oooooooooh! It sparkles!"

—the beads of water on her slime strands are like diamonds to her, and everybody feels her feeling at once, even Sandy—

"Ooooooooooh! It sparkles!"

—surfaced euphoric! euphorically garlanded in long greasy garlands of pond slime, the happiest slime freak in the West—

—and Babbs is euphoric for her—

"Gretchen Fetchin the Slime Queen!" he yells and waves his cane at the sky.

"Ooooooooh! It sparkles!"

"Gretchen Fetchin the Slime Queen!"

"It sparkles!"

"Gretchen Fetchin!"

And it is beautiful. Everybody goes manic and euphoric like a vast contact high, like they have all suddenly taken acid themselves. Kesey is in an athletic romp, tackling the ferns and other slimy greenery in the lake. Babbs and Paula—Gretchen Fetchin!—are yahooing at the sky. Hagen is feverishly filming it all, Sandy has a set of huge cables stretched out to the very edge of the lake, picking up the sound, Ron Bevirt is banging away with his camera. Babbs and Paula—Gretchen Fetchin!—and Kesey keep plunging out into the mucky innards of the lake.

"Come back!" Hagen the cameraman starts yelling. "You're out of range!"

But Babbs and Paula and Kesey can't hear him. They are cartwheeling further and further out into the paradise muck—

"It sparkles!"

"Gretchen Fetchin—Queen of the Slime!"

But meanwhile Hagen's Beauty Witch, in the contagion of the moment, has slipped to the refrigerator and taken some acid, and now she is outside of the bus on the desert sand wearing a black snakeskin blouse and a black mantle, with her long black hair coming down over it like in a pre-Raphaelite painting and a cosmic grin on her witch-white face, lying down on the desert, striking poses and declaiming in couplets. She's zonked out of her nut, but it's all in wild manic Elizabethan couplets:

"Methinks you need a gulp of grass
And so it quickly came to pass
You fell to earth with eely shrieking,
Wooing my heart, freely freaking!"

—and so forth. Well, she wins Hagen's manic heart right away, and soon he was wandered off from the Lake of the

Slime Euphoria and is in a wide-legged stance over her with the camera as she lies declaiming on the desert floor, camera zeroed in on her like she is Maria Montez in a love scene—and now the Beauty Witch is off on her trip for good. . . .

Back on the bus and off for Phoenix in the slime-euphoric certitude that they and the movie—The Movie!—many allegories of life—that they could not miss now. Hagen pressed on with the film, hour after hour in the bouncing innards of the bus. There were moments in the History of Film that broke everybody up. One was when they reached Phoenix. This was during the 1964 election excitement and they were in Barry Goldwater's home town, so they put a streamer on the bus reading: "A Vote for Barry is a Vote for Fun." And they put American flags up on the bus and Cassady drove the bus backward down the main drag of Phoenix while Hagen recorded it on film and the flags flew backward in the windstream. The citizens were suitably startled, outraged, delighted, nonplused, and would wheel around and start or else try to keep their cool by sidling glances like they weren't going to be impressed by any *weird shit*—and a few smiled in a frank way as if to say, I am with you—if only I could be with you!

The fact that they were all high on speed or grass, or so many combinations thereof that they couldn't keep track, made it seem like a great secret life. It was a great secret life. The befuddled citizens could only see the outward manifestations of the incredible stuff going on inside their skulls. They were all now characters in their own movies or the Big Movie. They took on new names and used them.

Steve Lambrecht was Zonker. Cassady was Speed Limit. Kesey was Swashbuckler. Babbs was Intrepid Traveler. Hagen, bouncing along with the big camera, soaring even while the bus roared, was Mal Function. Ron Bevirt had charge of all the equipment, the tools, wires, jacks, and stuff, and became known as Equipment Hassler, and then just Hassler. George Walker was Hardly Visible. And Paula Sundsten became . . . Gretchen Fetchin the Slime Queen, of course. . . .

A notebook!—for each of the new characters in The Movie, a plain child's notebook, and each character in this here movie can write in his notebook himself or other people can pick up the notebook and write in it—who knows who wrote what?—and in Gretchen Fetchin it says:

Bury them in slime!
She cried, flailing about the garden—
With a sprig of parsley clutched in
her hands—which had always been
clamped in her hands.

This is strange business,
Gets weirder all the time,
She said, wrapping some around
her finger, for we are always
moist in her hand . . . "Naturally," she
said, "The roots are deep."
That was no surprise, but she
was mildly curious to
know what the hell is

THAT
Whereupon he got very
clumsy, giggled confidentially,
and tripped over her shadow,
carrying them both into
an unaccountable adventure.

Barely a week out and already beautiful ebullient sexy Gretchen Fetchin the Slime Queen, Gretch, is *synched* in. Kesey, the very Swashbuckler himself, makes a play for her, and that should be that, but she looks at—Babbs—who tripped over her shadow!—Hmmmmmmmmm? So many shadows and shafts of Southwest sun bouncing in through the windows and all over the floor, over the benches over the bunk uprights bouncing out of the freaking roar of the engine bouncing two sets of Gretch eyes two sets of Babbs eyes, four sets of Gretch eyes four sets of Babbs eyes eight sets of Gretch eyes eight sets of Babbs eyes all grinning vibrating bouncing in among one another carrying them both into an unaccountable adventure, you understand. Kesey sulks a bit—Kesey himself—but the sulk bounces and breaks up into Southwestern sunballs. *Drivin' on dirt in Utah, a '46 Plymouth with an overhead cam,* says Cassady. The refrigerator door squeaks open, gurgle gurgle, this acid O.J. makes a body plumb smack his lips, Hagen and his Black Witch girl friend hook down a cup of acid orange juice apiece and Hagen's sweet face spirals, turning sweet Christian boy clockwise and sweet sly Screw Shack counter-clockwise, back and forth, and they disappear, bouncing, up the ladder, up through the turret hole and onto the roof where, under the mightily hulking sun of the Southwest and 70 miles an hour—Pretty soon Hagen is climbing back down the ladder and heading for the refrigerator and hooking down another cup of orange juice and smiling for all, Christian boy and Screw Shack sly, spiraling this way and that way—and climbing back up top the bus in order to—

MAL FUNCTION!
 If only I had $10, then we
could split ½ a Ritalin order
 with Margo—I eat
Ritalin like aspirin
 Now, let's charm Brooks Brothers—
impressed?

At night the goddamn bus still bouncing and the Southwest silvery blue coming in not exactly bouncing but slipping and sliding in shafts, sickly shit, and car beams and long crazy shadows from car beams sliding in weird bends over the inside, over the love bunk. The love bunk'll get you if you don't wash out. One shelf on the bunk has a sleeping bag on it and into this sleeping bag crawl whoever wants to make it, do your thing, bub, and right out front, and wail with it, and Sandy looks over and he can see a human . . . bobbing up and down in the sleeping bag with the car beams sliding over it and the motor roaring, the fabulous love bunk, and everyone—*synch*—can see that sleeping bag veritably filling up with sperm, the little devils swimming like mad in there in the muck, oozing into the cheap hairy shit they quilt the bag with, millions billions trillions of them, darting around, crafty little flagellants, looking to *score*, which is natural, and if any certified virgin of the face of the earth crawled into that sleeping bag for a nap after lunch she would be a hulking knocked-up miracle inside of three minutes—but won't this goddamn *bouncing* ever stop—

Dropouts with a Mission

Newsweek

The following article from a February 1967 edition of *Newsweek* is a description of the hallucinogen-inspired hippie subculture that had just emerged in the United States, most notably in the Haight-Ashbury district of San Francisco, California. Young, long-haired, and brightly clothed, the hippies reject political activism, war, and monogamy while embracing communal living, LSD, and mysticism. While sympathetic observers appreciate the hippies' spontaneity and honesty, *Newsweek* cautions that their drug-taking, anti-intellectualism, and tendency to attract disturbed individuals and runaways threaten their utopian aspirations.

They smile and call themselves a new race. They want to change the United States from within—by means of a vague regimen of all-embracing love. They are nonviolent, mystical, bizarre. Psychedelic drugs are their instant passport to Nirvana, a euphoric disdain for anything "square" is their most common bond. Like the beatniks of the '50s, they are in the long tradition of Bohemia: seeking a vision of totally free life. They are, of course, the hippies.

A fine example of their communal style occurred Jan. 14 in San Francisco, where some 10,000 long-tressed hippies of both sexes, and various fellow-trippers, met at Golden Gate Park for the world's first "Human Be-In." They wore blowsy furs, fresh flowers, jangling beads, floppy-brimmed hats, even

Indian war paint. They waved sticks of burning incense, swirled abstractly designed banners, tooted on fifes and recorders. There under the warm sun with the faithful was the whole range of the hippie hierarchy. Poet Allen Ginsberg tried to lead the crowd in a Hare Krishna swami chant; Timothy Leary, headmaster of the LSD school, delivered a plea to "turn on, tune in and drop out," and Pig-Pen, the pop organist whose gaudy sweatshirts have become standard apparel for hundreds of teen-age girls, invoked the hippies via another favorite idiom—rock music.

But nobody paid much attention to such celebrities. In gentle anarchy—there was little pushing or elbowing—people twirled around a maypole, clapped, laughed, embraced and danced to the music of such groups as the Grateful Dead and the Quicksilver Messenger Service.

It was a love feast, a psychedelic picnic, a hippie happening. Among the images that flickered across the scene: a parachutist dropped from the sky and disappeared into the crowd; a bearded boy in denim, muttering, shouting and clenching his fists, threw himself on the ground and bystanders patted him reassuringly on the shoulder; a wide-eyed child of 3 with a "Frodo Lives" button (after the good elf in the Tolkien stories) surveyed the scene dispassionately.

Sick Society

"Our attitude is strictly laissez-faire," explained Jerry Garcia, leader of the Grateful Dead, who has earned the nickname "Captain Trips" because of his interest in LSD excursions.

If the first Human Be-In didn't go anywhere in particular, it nonetheless confirmed one fact: San Francisco has arrived as the hub of the hippie world. Other cities have their hip societies. New York's East Village claims a large population; Los Angeles hippies are a familiar fixture on Sunset Strip. In their 20s or early 30s, often with an itch to be artists, hippies wander from Amsterdam to Afghanistan. They are seldom actively political, inevitably hard-up for cash, always dead set against every culture but their own. Although they are few in number, their network is worldwide.

"The hippies are a barometer of our sick society," says a California sociologist. "They are dropouts who are turned off by the wars, poverty, political phoniness and the 'game' they see around them."

Nowhere does hippiehood flourish as it does in San Francisco. "There isn't any place where I can live as well and as comfortably—and just as totally as I can here," said 28-year-old Og Sing, a world-traveling hippie.

Nobody is sure how many hippies there are in San Francisco. But a source who is familiar with the distribution pattern of LSD, the psychedelic drug that activates the hip world, estimates there are about 5,000 full-time San Francisco hippies and somewhere between 25,000 and 30,000 weekend hippies, who can be loosely defined as teen-agers only sporadically switched-on.

Far-Out Wares

The important hippie stronghold is the Haight-Ashbury district, a ten- by fifteen-block area just east of Golden Gate Park. Until a year ago, it was simply another cluster of decaying Victorian frame houses. Then, in February 1966, the Psychedelic Shop opened at 1535 Haight Street and began displaying its wares of far-out books, magazines, records and amulets. This was the signal for the hippies to move in. Now there are 40 new shops and cottage industries, banded together in their own trade association, the Haight-Ashbury Independent Proprietors (HIP). HIP includes such emporiums as the Blushing Peony Skinnidippin and the Chickie P. Garbanzo Bead and Storm Door Co., Ltd., offering sandals, marijuana pipes and handmade jewelry.

Hippies seem to float, serene, smiling, detached, through the Haight-Ashbury area—chatting on a corner, perhaps sitting atop a lamppost, enacting a kind of slow-motion circus. In fact, they sport what is probably the most clownish array of clothing ever collected in a single community: cowboy hats, sombreros, tall stovepipes, aluminum ties, silk frock coats, Naval uniforms with the original buttons replaced with ones reading "Nirvana Now," Mexican blanket vests, denim vests, anklets, bracelets, boots, bare feet.

But way-out clothing is only a minor appurtenance of the hippie life. More significant is their philosophy, endlessly thrashed out in colloquies at the pads of the more admired leaders of the Movement. *Newsweek*'s Hendrik Hertzberg recently visited just such a pad—the five-room apartment of Michael Bowen, a 29-year-old painter and one of the more renowned citizens of the hip world. Like many hippie house-holders, Bowen has a meditation room—walls covered with gaily colored Hindu tapestries and light filtering through a window covered with rice paper. There, while Hertzberg listened, hippies sat on floor mats, offering their opinions on what's wrong with the world and how hippies are changing it. His report:

"For the first time, men and women are becoming friends again," offered Laurie Baxer, 21, a doe-like blonde. "Just friends. And that's a very nice feeling—to be able to really communicate with somebody, not with a man or a woman but with a person who obviously is a man or a woman. Certain external things, such as short hair, long hair or manner of dress, no longer make the difference. We view it as a kind of blasphemy that a man is masculine because he has short hair and feminine because he has long hair."

For the hippies, sex is not a matter of great debate, because as far as they are concerned the sexual revolution is accomplished. There are no hippies who believe in chastity, or look askance at marital infidelity or see even marriage itself as a virtue. Physical love is a delight—to be chewed upon as often and freely as a handful of sesame seeds. "Sex is psychedelic," said Gary Goldhill, 38, an Englishman who gave up radio scriptwriting to live as a painter in the Haight-Ashbury area. "And, in all psychedelic things, sex is very important."

Artistic

Characteristic of the hippies is a sharp delineation of the roles of the sexes, with women voluntarily choosing traditional feminine chores. "More chicks now are getting into sewing, making their own clothes, and getting into leatherwork, so they can make moccasins and sandals," said a classically beautiful, sandy-haired 24-year-old woman who uses only a first name— Martine. "I spend all day cooking, sewing, straightening the house. I used to think I wanted to be an artist. But now, I am."

Like many hippies, Martine is deeply interested in macrobiotic food (a diet under which one New York girl starved to death not long ago). The macrobiotic diet is an offshoot of Buddhism and involves avoiding foods that are too yin or too yang in preference for those that are in between, such as rice and cereal. "I believe that it makes your life more beautiful," said Martine.

The hippies have also been experimenting with new kinds of family systems. In the Haight-Ashbury it is not unusual to find two dozen people living together as an extended family unit. The community itself is organized almost as a tribe composed of a series of clans. Goldhill offered an explanation of why the borderline of a hippie family is not as sharp as among the squares. "Usually it's man and woman against the world," he said. "You're brought up in a competitive society and you're taught to grab first because if you don't everyone else will. In the Haight-Ashbury many families live together, because it's a cooperative and not a competitive thing."

Mind Blasts

The subject of language—and the hippies' suspicion of it— came up for discussion at Bowen's apartment. Since the hippie esthetic emphasizes total, instant sensory involvement, they seem productive in rock music, abstract-light shows, experimental films and painting—but unproductive in literature. The group agreed but Michael McClure, one of the few serious hippie writers and author of "The Beard"—a play about a love affair between Jean Harlow and Billy the Kid—predicted there would be a real and radical hippie literature. McClure said he had just written a novel. "I wrote it as fast as I could type, in mind blasts," he explained. "Like I'd take a picture in my mind and I'd type the picture as fast as I could, regardless of whether it was a one-page picture or a ten-page picture, and then go on to the next picture."

How do hippies support themselves? The largest single employer of hippies is the U.S. Post Office, and the sight of a bearded mailman with a peace button on the lapel of his uniform has become a common one in San Francisco. Another source of income is "dealing" or selling drugs, usually marijuana, LSD and "speed" (methedrine), since hippies generally leave heroin alone. A dope dealer's income frequently supports a whole group of people. Some hippies also depend on a subsidy from home. At the same time, many do have jobs in the arts—as poster designers, actors, dancers and rock musicians.

Joyously

"When we get enough money to live for a couple of weeks, unless we're doing something creative, we'll probably stop work," explained Goldhill. It's not because we're lazy but because we think there are far more valuable things to do with our lives. We think that to waste life doing repetitive jobs is blasphemy, when to live joyously and creatively is to live close to God. God is the root and therefore his creation was done for Himself, and something you do for yourself is play. Creation is play."

The more introspective hippies are groping for a religion. To them, whatever its vague tenets, it is religion that is always first-hand, personal and immediate because it is based on revelation through LSD. Virtually every hippie has taken LSD, which means that every one has had a "vision." It is certainly questionable whether this vision—the peering into one's self while under the influence of LSD—reveals any truth or simply subjects the user to a fantasy in which he runs a grave risk of psychosis.

But for the hippie the trip is a mystical experience, and it is this that gives the distinctive tone to the hip world and distinguishes it from earlier Bohemian societies. The style of San Francisco's North Beach beatniks of the late '50s was worldly and secular. The style of the Haight-Ashbury hippies is religious and ethereal. In some hippies the style has spawned a messianic zeal to reform the square world—a rather ambitious goal considering the general reluctance of suburbia to be psychedelicized.

While he sat in his meditation room, Michael Bowen described an arcane brotherhood of which he is a leader known as the "Psychedelic Rangers." "The Rangers," says Bowen, "are for everything good. It's very supersecret. They range around and straighten the rot wherever they find it." One of the Rangers' prophecies: "The psychedelic baby eats the cybernetic monster."

"The psychedelic baby is what is occurring here in the United States, with people taking LSD, dropping out, making these communities and so forth," explained Bowen. "The psychedelic baby coming in contact with the cybernetic monster will devour it and by doing so the psychedelic baby will have the strength of the electronic civilization. That doesn't mean back to savagery. It doesn't mean we're going to tear down all the computer systems. It's only a question of the mind being tuned enough, so that it's involved in making things better. And this will result in a civilization that is super-beautiful. We're out to build an electric Tibet."

All Insane

At this point, Bowen looked around the room and a grin crossed his face. "Shall we sing 'We Are All Insane'?" he suggested. He began singing it, to the tune of "We Shall Overcome," and everybody joined in. After a few choruses, it trailed off and Bowen and Martine began to chant the Kirtan, a Hindu prayer: "Hare Krishna, Hare Krishna, Krishna Krishna, Hare Hare, Hare Rama, Hare Rama, Rama Rama, Hare Hare." Over and over again they chanted it, for twenty minutes. Later, as the gathering broke up, Bowen explained: "The continuous repetition of the proper words gets you high."

There is, of course, a low as well as a high side to the hippie phenomenon. In the Haight-Ashbury district, seriously disturbed people and teen-age runaways make up a sizable fringe of the Movement. Equally unsettling is the incipient anti-intellectualism of the hippies—to say nothing of the dangers of drug-taking. The hippie's euphoria is too often bought at the price of his intellectual and critical faculties. Indeed, the hippie's life is so lacking in competitive tension and tangible goals that it risks an overpowering boredom. Faced by these shortcomings, some younger hippies may well grow disillusioned, clip their hair and rejoin the squares. If they do, the more sympathetic observers of the hippie scene suggest that at best they may bring with them a worthwhile residue: spontaneity, honesty and appreciation for the wonder of life.

The Media and the Abuse of LSD

Donald B. Louria

The mainstream media are largely to blame for the popularity of LSD among youth, maintains Donald B. Louria in this 1967 essay. Reporters and popular writers have focused on the pleasures of hallucinogens while greatly downplaying their enormous dangers. Moreover, writes Louria, some opportunists claim that hallucinogens enhance sexual feelings, while others profit from the sale of LSD-inspired art and motifs. Such publicity only induces young people to try a drug that may permanently damage their lives, he contends. Louria concludes that a combination of stronger laws, education, and family love could curb the abuse of hallucinogens. Louria is the former chair of preventative medicine at New Jersey Medical School. When he wrote this essay, he was chair of the New York County Medical Society's narcotics subcommittee, and the possession of LSD had not yet been outlawed.

There can be little doubt that the communications media bear a heavy responsibility for the spread of LSD abuse. Over and over they have emphasized the ecstasies and hedonistic values of LSD and underemphasized its enormous dangers. All too frequently sensationalism rather than facts and a balanced approach have characterized their efforts. At times reporters have carefully researched the dangers of LSD and then deliberately ignored or minimized them in the published articles.

Since virtually every major magazine, newspaper and tele-

Donald B. Louria, "The Abuse of LSD," *LSD, Man, and Society,* edited by Richard C. DeBold and Russell C. Leaf. Middletown, CT: Wesleyan University Press, 1967. Copyright © 1967 by Wesleyan University. Reproduced by permission.

vision network has examined the LSD phenomenon, these un-critical and distorted reports have reached a large number of susceptible young persons. In every group of high-school or college students, there are some individuals who would never take LSD, some who could not be prevented from trying it and others, usually the majority, who are potentially susceptible to the inadvertent blandishments of the communications media. It is the latter group that is most likely to be harmed by such irresponsible publicity.

Misleading Statements

The most recent claim that terrifying LSD experiences can be immediately aborted and treated successfully with certain tranquillizers is the latest example of unsubstantiated reports being transmuted into valid facts and transmitted to the public. It is indeed true that under *controlled* circumstances administration of chlorpromazine, together with other supportive measures, *may* abort untoward reactions, but these ministrations are less likely to be successful in uncontrolled situations. Indeed, at Bellevue Hospital, patients are treated routinely with chlorpromazine, but this has not prevented one in six from requiring prolonged hospitalization. Similarly no tranquillizer helps the individual who in a sudden panic jumps out a window or in front of a train. Yet these reports, given wide publicity by an eager press, are being used to justify indiscriminate use of LSD.

Perhaps the most reprehensible and misleading statement regarding LSD is the claim that it is a potent aphrodisiac. This claim is made by the avowed proselytizers, and more than any other single statement is effective in recruiting new converts to the LSD cult. LSD proponents insist that sexual relations under the influence of LSD are a spectacular, unmatched experience. They, of course, neglect to mention that the overwhelming majority of those taking LSD have no interest in sex, preferring their solipsistic trance, and that others who have taken LSD and attempted intercourse have found it impossible to consummate. Furthermore, the person responsible for the statement [Timothy Leary], when specifically challenged on this point in a public debate in the fall of 1966, said that the statement was misinterpreted and that he in fact meant that LSD induces love in its most ethereal sense, but has no beneficial effect on casual or promiscuous physical sexual behavior.

Yet the myth, almost surely deliberately promulgated, will persist and will coax unsuspecting young people to try a drug that has the capacity to affect adversely their lives acutely, chronically or even permanently. The same myth has been utilized by proponents of marijuana, cocaine and the amphetamines. For those who would proselytize, sex is always better under the drug that they illicitly use.

The LSD Mystique

There is, of course, an additional inducement for some to continue the publicity and to disseminate the myths. These individuals are involved in secondary gain, which takes the form either of personal notoriety or of monetary reward. The LSD proponents hawk their psychedelic wares in hard-cover books, paperbacks, pamphlets and speeches. Furthermore, they openly admit that there is virtually unlimited commercial applicability for the psychedelic movement; theatre shows, discothèques, cabarets, restaurants, motion pictures, *etc.* with psychedelic motif are providing handsome financial returns. For these entrepreneurs, the use of LSD *per se* is not mandatory, but the LSD mystique, together with the myths and the publicity, is a necessary component that reminds the audience that their money is being spent on a psychedelic experience that mimics the hedonistic effects of the drug. Inevitably, some of those who enjoy the non-drug psychedelic experience will be inveigled by the overt and surreptitious inducements to try the real thing. To quote Dr. Sidney Cohen: "Some of the young in mind who obtain the black market material will casually take it under dubious conditions and without the necessary controls. Sooner or later they will find themselves caught in the grip of pure horror. With LSD the kicks can go both ways."

The Abuse of Other Potent Hallucinogens

LSD is only one of many moderately to markedly potent hallucinogenic agents. A small number are known in Europe, Asia and Africa, and Latin America is a veritable hallucinogenic cornucopia. Some of those currently available in the United States are listed in Table I. Of these, dimethyltryptamine (DMT) offers the greatest potential for widespread abuse, because it is the most readily manufactured. Usually smoked, it can also be snuffed, ingested or injected.

TABLE I

Potent Hallucinogens Illicitly Used in the United States

Lysergic acid diethylamide (LSD-25)
Psilocybin
Mescaline
Dimethyltryptamine (DMT)
Bufotenine
Hashish

. . . Hallucinogens [are] found in other parts of the world. For the most part these are used by primitive peoples in religious rites, in warfare, in tribal ceremonies, for purposes of divination or for transient escape from the deprivations and appalling poverty that characterize their daily existence. It seems unlikely that any of these will be directly used in the United States in their present forms, but the active components of some of them have been or will soon be defined chemically. These synthetic hallucinogens will then be available for illicit manufacture and indiscriminate use. This is in fact what happened with dimethyltryptamine and psilocybin; the former constitutes an active principle in several hallucinogenic substances of Latin

America, and the latter is an active component of the sacred hallucinogenic Mexican mushroom *Psilocybe mexicana*. In each case it was the synthetic drug rather than the naturally occurring agent that was illicitly used in the United States.

Thus LSD can be regarded only as one head of a psychedelic hydra; eliminate it, and we shall surely face other similar agents. The therapy for this abuse must consequently be general, not parochial, and must be multifaceted. If we as a society make the judgement, as indeed we must, that proliferation of these drugs and indiscriminate use of them under non-medical aegis are dangerous to the individual and potentially dangerous to society, then we have a right to demand appropriate controls.

Addressing Drug Abuse

The following would appear to be essential components of any attack on hallucinogen abuse:

a. Laws restricting supply by imposing severe penalties for illicit importation, manufacture or sale.

b. Laws making illegal possession a misdemeanor. This conceivably could merely drive LSD and similar drugs underground, make them more enticing and thus expand illicit use; however, it is more likely that such laws, combined with dissemination of knowledge about physical and mental risks, would persuade some potentially susceptible individuals to eschew use of potent and potentially dangerous hallucinogens.

c. Laws proscribing possession of precursors of hallucinogens such as LSD and mescaline. If lysergic acid and trimethoxyphenyl-acetonitrile were not available, the abuse of lysergic acid diethylamide or mescaline would almost surely decline. Of the currently used potent hallucinogens, only DMT is so easy to manufacture that its precursors could not be interdicted.

d. Education. Young people are, for the most part, eminently educable. Vigorous, continuous and impeccably honest education about the dangers of potent hallucinogens should do more than laws to reduce the numbers influenced by the psychedelic proselytizers.

e. Strengthening the family unit. It perhaps seems trite to emphasize that deterioration of the cohesiveness of the family unit has resulted in the presence in society of an increasing number of insecure, unhappy and confused young persons. Such individuals either do not have the strength to resist the lure of LSD or may actively seek the drug as a manifestation of inherent personality defects. Surely a strong and loving family unit is far more likely to produce young persons strong enough to separate wants from needs, to reject drug proselytizers and to seek constructive solutions to their problems. If the family unit is not revitalized, efforts at prevention by a combination of laws and education will surely be only partially successful.

The Decline of the Psychedelic Movement

Lester Grinspoon and James B. Bakalar

The hallucinogen-inspired counterculture degenerated by the end of the 1960s, write Lester Grinspoon and James B. Bakalar in the following selection. Hippies ultimately could not live up to their own ideals. Countercultural enclaves became increasingly populated with phony "weekend" hippies, runaways, drug addicts, mentally ill people, and con artists, and psychedelic drugs held no power to sustain a genuine community, the authors explain. Most hippies eventually returned to their middle-class lifestyles, with some adopting the disciplines of Eastern religion and meditation. Grinspoon is an associate professor emeritus of psychiatry at Harvard Medical School and the author of numerous articles and books, including *Marihuana: The Forbidden Medicine*. Bakalar is a lecturer in the department of psychiatry at Harvard Medical School and editor of the *Harvard Mental Health Letter*.

The hippie movement constituted the mass following of the psychedelic ideology. It began to gather force around 1965 and reached its height between 1967 and 1969. Although the matter was often obscured for tactical reasons, there is no doubt that the initiating element, the sacrament, the symbolic center, the source of group identity in hippie lives was the psychedelic drug trip. To drop out, you had to turn on. It was not a question of how often the drugs were used; sometimes once was enough, and many people experienced a kind of cultural contact high without taking drugs at all. . . .

The Purpose of Hippie Style

The hippie movement in its visions combined a theoretical benevolence and gentleness with an interest in communitarian experiments, the occult, magic, exotic ritual, and mysticism. It borrowed its crazy-quilt of ideas from depth psychology, oriental religion, anarchism, American Indian lore, and the Romantic and Beat literary current of inspired spontaneity. Middle-class young people, provided with a childhood free of the most obvious forms of coercion and made self-conscious by the adolescent subculture and the youth consumer market that supplied it, were unwilling to submit to what they saw as the hypocrisies and rigidities demanded by adult jobs and roles, the unfreedom of adult life; a society worried about unemployment was willing to delay their entry into the job market and prolong their adolescence. The implicit purpose of the hippie style was to prolong the freedom and playfulness of childhood as far as possible into adulthood: to make the culture a youth culture. They rejected the accepted social definitions of reason, progress, knowledge, and even reality; they proclaimed their abandonment of the egocentrism and compulsiveness of the technological world view. American society was seen as a dehumanizing, commercialized air-conditioned nightmare, meanly conformist in its manners and morals, hypocritical in its religion, murderous and repressive in its politics; it outlawed the liberating psychedelic drugs and approved of enslaving alcohol and nicotine. A transformed way of life would be built on the intimations provided by LSD, the "mind detergent" that purged the psyche and midwifed a personal rebirth as the first step toward a new form of community. . . .

The alleged enemy was conformist society, the straight

world, adults, medical authorities, the government, the law, and so on—a situation well defined in the title of a book by Nicholas von Hoffman: *We Are the People Our Parents Warned Us Against.* But things were not so simple. America confronted the hippies with a mixture of attraction and revulsion summed up in the two public faces of the lazy, dirty, hedonistic, promiscuous, and parasitical dope fiends and the radiantly angelic product of the love generation. The hippies made conventional society anxious but also touched its imagination. After all, some of them were the sons and daughters of its pillars. Favorable and unfavorable publicity in the mass media were equally effective in spreading the use of psychedelic drugs. Paeans to the gentleness, peaceableness, and sexual openness of the flower children made recruits for the drug culture; reports of suicides, fatal falls, or psychotic reactions were discounted as establishment propaganda, and it was even said (especially by [Timothy] Leary) that scare publicity and medical mishandling *caused* most bad drug reactions. Cops-and-robbers stories about drug arrests contributed to the exhilarating sense of forbidden adventure. Students surveyed at a

 THE HISTORY OF DRUGS

The Downside of Psychedelia

Does the psychedelic experience really have to be offered to the public in the form of bizarre shows? Do the psychedelic people have to live in squalid ghettos? Does their conversation have to be a rapid-fire rap of slogans and meaningless declarations of "love"? Does LSD still have to be used so excessively and so carelessly; do freakouts have to be regular occurrences . . . ? Do interpersonal relationships among acidheads have to be so shallow, so shortlived? Must the leaders deliberately foster distrust between age groups? Do cheating and stealing have to be the rule among acid dealers?

Lisa Bieberman, *New Republic*, August 5, 1967.

high school in California in 1967, when asked whom they would trust as the narrator of an anti-LSD film, answered "no one": a common effect of adverse drug publicity in the sixties on young people who understood how much hypocrisy, displacement, and projection went into adult condemnations. And yet it was partly the way some adults flattered them as spiritual and social innovators that made young drug users so confident of their judgment. Some professional people—sociologists, psychologists, journalists, clergymen—were so excited by the hippies' proclamations of messianic transcendence and social revolution that they abandoned their own judgment and invested disappointed hopes for drastic and immediate change in a movement that made promises far beyond its capacities.

Repression and Decline

Amid the mixture of hostility and approbation that greeted the hippies and their drugs, the law hesitated for a while and then came down on the side of repression. In the early days psychedelic drugs were not treated with the peculiar moralistic severity reserved for substances classified as "narcotics" (including, ironically, the much milder marihuana). Until 1963 LSD, mescaline, and psilocybin were easy to obtain for clinical and experimental research; and until 1966 there were no state or federal criminal penalties for unauthorized possession, manufacture, and sale. Only after 1966, when Sandoz took its LSD off the market in response to the new laws and the new public atmosphere, was most of the LSD in circulation manufactured in illicit laboratories. Under the present comprehensive federal drug law, which was enacted in 1970, most "hallucinogens" including marihuana are classified as drugs with a high potential for abuse and no current medical use; possession for personal use is a misdemeanor, unauthorized manufacture or sale a felony. State laws are similar to the federal law.

One familiar effect of illegality is a decline in drug purity and quality. A common complaint, voiced by [Ken] Kesey, Michael Hollingshead (the man who introduced LSD to Leary), and other connoisseurs, is that the illicit drug available after 1966 was not the same as pure Sandoz LSD: the trip provided by illicit LSD was a chaotic, mind-shattering, physically and emotionally exhausting roller coaster ride instead of a serene cruise with a clear view of Reality. The decline of the psychedelic movement has even been attributed to the loss of its sacrament. . . .

There is now a stable pattern: a small but not negligible minority of young people in their teens and early twenties, including a relatively large proportion of the undergraduates at academically selective colleges, take LSD several times over a period of a year or two and then stop. Very few use it continually or go on using it for long. . . .

Psychedelic drugs, then, are still with us, but the psychedelic movement has disappeared. Its unity proved to be spurious, its staying power a false hope. . . .

Psychedelic drugs could sustain cults but not a culture; the hippies could not live up to their own hopes any more than they could justify the fears of their enemies. From the start the movement was amorphous, muddled, with great variations in participation and commitment. Occasional masters or gurus, often older men, provided philosophical justifications and political guidance; a few hippies were organized into communes and tribes and manned the institutions of the culture; but many were dropouts, some of them runaways, who drifted into the life with no clear conception of what they wanted or were rejecting and drifted out again in a few years after succeeding or failing in the transition to adulthood; and an even larger number were never more than "weekend" or "plastic" hippies, tourists wearing native garb whose idea of the scene was derived from psychedelic travel posters. Most of the young people who might once have been called hippies by the mass media or even described themselves that way never grasped much more than an opportunity to find drugs, sex, excitement, freedom from rules and restrictions, or, most touchingly, a home and family away from their homes and families. They were [in Hofmann's words], "the simple hippies, the stray teeny-boppers, the runaways, the summer dropouts—the micro-organisms without power of locomotion that hung in the heavy water pool of Haight-Ashbury waiting for the more complex creatures to inhale them into their mouths and ingest them into their bellies where they could be food"—and, if they did not find their way out, potential victims for a man like [cult leader and murderer] Charles Manson. . . .

Exploitation and Disillusion

As the disintegration proceeded, pieces picked themselves up and moved off in various directions, which can be represented symbolically by Methedrine, Marxism (or Maoism), Marihuana, and Meditation. Progressing from psychedelic drugs to intravenous injection of Methedrine (methamphetamine) and then addiction to depressants (alcohol, barbiturates, and heroin) was one form of the descent into despair and misery that revealed how much in the drug culture had always been pathological. The high language about love and community emanating from the few articulate leaders admired by sympathetic observers obscured a great deal of sordid reality. The hippie world's benign tolerance for eccentricity, its refusal to judge, make rules, or exclude, and its programmatic lack of discipline had attracted unstable persons who not only would not but could not make lives for themselves in straight society—from adolescents in turmoil to borderline psychotics like Charles Manson and antisocial characters like the Hell's Angels. The drug culture had no resources to protect itself against those who joined it to disguise justify, or alleviate their disturbed conditions. For the same reasons it was easily corrupted by drug dealers' profiteering and co-opted by commercial exploitation of its superficial symbols. . . .

The drug culture's downward path is retraced in detail in *Love Needs Care*, David E. Smith's and John Luce's chronicle of the rise and decline of the Haight-Ashbury hippie community from 1965 to 1969. Haight-Ashbury became a center of the counterculture in 1965 with the opening of a psychedelic shop selling drug paraphernalia. It was enriched by an influx from the nearby North Beach area of Beat Generation fame, and attracted the attention of the mass media after the Be-In or Gathering of the Tribes in Golden Gate Park in January 1967. The press spread rumors that 100,000 migrants would be coming that summer. It was a self-fulfilling prophecy that attracted many young people to the dubiously named Summer of Love, sometimes regarded as the flood tide of the drug culture. If it was, the ebb began immediately and was precipitous; by January of 1968 most of the flower children had abandoned the scene and it was dominated by speed freaks, addicts, alcoholics, motorcycle hoodlums, and the teenage runaways and schizoid or inadequate personalities they preyed on. Hepatitis, bronchitis, venereal disease, decayed teeth, malnutrition, and untreated cuts and burns, always problems in urban hippie enclaves, had become pervasive.

Haight Street served as a kind of laboratory that provided advance signals of the consequences of tendencies implicit in the movement from the start. The early rural communes, for example, unable to exclude or reject anyone and incapable of managing their affairs, tended to fall apart in chaos. The Woodstock Rock Festival of 1969 and the talk of a Woodstock Nation for years afterward seemed to prove that the counterculture still had some life. But Woodstock was mainly a gathering of "plastic hippies": middle-class young people on vacation, many of whom lived with their parents or in college dormitories. The Altamont Rock Festival of 1970, with its murderous culmination, was sometimes proclaimed to be the counterculture's final self-inflicted blow. But the problems had been inherent from the start. Charles Manson had been taking LSD with his "family" in Haight-Ashbury during the Summer of

Love, and the summer of Woodstock was also the summer of the Tate and LaBianca murders. . . . Everything about Manson, including the form his delusions took, was a perfect malicious caricature of hippie beliefs and the hippie way of life. . . .

LSD Fails as a Pleasure Drug

Radical politics or addictive drugs absorbed only a few of the people who had temporarily assumed the habits and language of the counterculture; most of them returned to more or less conventional lives. As usual after a conversion, there was much backsliding. Even for those who did not abandon them, psychedelic drugs ceased to imply cultural radicalism. LSD was taken more casually, for pleasure, without apocalyptic expectations; often its more profound effects were deliberately suppressed:

> There are like six people sitting in a room tripping, and grooving on the pretty colors, and suddenly Jane starts getting into something heavy. She begins to realize that acid is a bigger thing than just seeing colors, and she begins to get deep into it and get frightened. Then somebody looks over and grins and says, "Whassa matta, Jane, you freaking out?" And either she snaps back into seeing the colors thing or she gets real frightened and never takes acid again.

But, as this quotation [from Harrison Pope's *Voices from the Drug Culture*] indicates, LSD was not a reliable pleasure drug: ecstasy is not fun. People who used psychedelic drugs mainly for what they defined as pleasure tended to stop sooner than those who had more serious and complex purposes. Illicit drug users looking for something that would not disrupt their normal routines returned to substances like marihuana and cocaine, which have reliably euphoric effects and do riot alter consciousness too much. Both have become increasingly acceptable as everyday social drugs; they are used simply to feel good, and not as a source of cultural identity. The magazine *High Times* is the *Playboy* of these new drug users. Despite some half-hearted counterculture rhetoric, its casual tone is very different from the rage and exaltation of the drug-culture press of the 1960s, and its readers no more constitute a sub-culture than do readers of *Gourmet* or whiskey drinkers. Psy-chedelic drugs play a relatively small part in their lives.

Everything is back to normal, then; but normality itself is different, and not only in the increasing acceptability of mari-huana as a pleasure drug. As the epithet "mind detergent" im-plies, in some circumstances LSD had a kind of brainwashing power; it could induce the feeling of having achieved a new identity through death and rebirth of the self. Even after this feeling faded, it often seemed that nothing would ever be quite the same again. The psychedelic voyage, like any adventure, changed the traveler. There were subtle differences in the sen-sibilities and interests of LSD users who turned off and dropped back in; they can be symbolized by Meditation, the fourth direction we have named for former followers of the psychedelic movement. . . .

A Turn to the East

Psychedelic drugs opened to mass tourism mental territories previously explored only by small parties of particularly intre-pid adventurers, mainly religious mystics. Most of the tourists simply returned with a memory of having seen something im-portant but no idea how to interpret it or incorporate it into their lives. But some decided to make their own attempts at ex-ploration without drugs, and they discovered that religious traditions had the best maps—especially the religions of India. The drugs whetted metaphysical appetites that Eastern reli-gion promised to satisfy. This project had great advantages over the drug culture in seriousness and permanence. Eastern gurus were relatively immune to the curiosity of the mass me-dia or condescending sociological expertise: they were neither sensational enough (since sex and drugs were not involved) nor easily subject to analysis on Western terms. Their rules, prohibitions, and insistence on arduous training were a relief to recruits weary of the drug culture's indiscipline and its anarchy of standards. Young people who had never learned self-discipline or even considered it important now discovered that it could order and enrich their lives; this may have mattered more than any of the specific spiritual techniques in maintaining a sense of community and psychological stability.

There were other factors as well. One perceptive observer has identified a common goal of *detoxification* on the journey to the East. To realize the ideals of simplicity and naturalness suggested but not achieved by the drug culture, it was necessary to get rid of technical aids that were seen as impure and ultimately in some sense poisonous. Many of those who turned to Eastern disciplines came to regard drugs as pollutants that overload the senses, distract the mind, and prevent the user from attaining the goals they allow him to glimpse. They were seen as dangerous and somehow fraudulent, artificial in a bad sense, like many other chemicals in the air of industrial society. People who now sought spontaneity and self-transcendence in all their experience could no longer tolerate confining them to unusual chemically induced states, especially ones that depended on drug technology. So doubts about Western science and industry already present in the drug culture, as well as the concern for purity and wholeness represented by the ecology movement, led to a rejection of psychedelic drugs.

CHAPTER FOUR

Contemporary Views on Hallucinogens

The Renewed Popularity of Psychedelic Drugs

Eugene Taylor

Liberal attitudes about recreational drug use and an increased curiosity about spirituality, psychology, and alternative consciousness led to a resurgence of interest in hallucinogens in the 1990s, writes Eugene Taylor in the following selection. The psychedelic revival is especially evident among people under the age of thirty, whose drugs of choice include marijuana and Ecstasy, a synthetic cross between an amphetamine and a hallucinogen. Physician-supervised use is also emerging as researchers explore the therapeutic potential of hallucinogens in psychotherapy, alcohol and drug addiction therapy, and AIDS and cancer treatment. Taylor is a lecturer in psychiatry at the Harvard University Medical School and the author of *A Psychology of Spiritual Healing* and *Shadow Culture: Psychology and Spirituality in America.*

Three decades after the late psychologist [Timothy Leary] advised a generation to turn on and tune in to LSD and other psychedelics, people are now doing it in droves. The difference is these days no one's dropping out. They don't have to. The world has turned. The goal of psychedelic use, psychospiritual awakening—looking inward, risking chaos, and struggling to overcome our lower nature in order to grasp at higher reali-

Eugene Taylor, "Psychedelics: The Second Coming," *Psychology Today*, vol. 29, July/August 1996, pp. 56–60. Copyright © 1996 by Sussex Publishers, Inc. Reproduced by permission.

ties—has the firm endorsement of that bellwether of cultural institutions, the bestseller list.

Increasingly, expansion of awareness seems a necessary condition for everyday life, not a mode of disconnection. That's why a significant number of Americans are now living with the alternative realities originally explored through psychedelic use. Environmental awareness has developed into a whole new movement called ecopsychology, defined as a spiritual consciousness of the earth. A holistic approach to wellness has moved center stage, along with interest in healthy foods, and physical fitness. Meanwhile, hypnosis, meditation, yoga, and biofeedback—all ways to alter one's consciousness—are now moving onto the national health care agenda as new forms of inexpensive, preventive self-administered medicine.

Psychospiritual Awakening

Psychospiritual awakening has become the watchword of a new psychology. None other than Aldous Huxley echoed such sentiments when, quoting the English poet William Blake, he said, "If the doors of perception were cleansed, everything would appear to man as it is, infinite." That was in 1954, in *The Doors of Perception*, a work that provided the first hint of the psychedelic revolution yet to come.

Psychedelics—the word itself—was coined in 1956 by the British psychiatrist Humphry Osmond and refers to the "mind-altering" properties of naturally occurring hallucinogenic plant substances such as marijuana (a common weed), psilocybin (a cow patty mushroom), peyote (a cactus flower), and LSD (a common bread mold). All can currently be found in parts of the U.S. with a little earnest looking in the wilderness.

Within a few years of Huxley's book, millions of people began experimenting with these substances. Garage laboratories manufacturing LSD sprouted everywhere and people began growing marijuana in their backyards.

"Psychedelic" soon became synonymous with journeys into

seemingly uncharted regions of inner experience, the expansion of consciousness, transcendence, and self-knowledge on a grand scale. It stood for altogether new forms of social experimentation in everything from dress and music to sex and civil rights.

Then, almost as suddenly as they had appeared, psychedelics disappeared. Legal measures drove them underground, where their use thrived. But the true products of the revolution, such as new definitions of the family, redefined gender roles, and the revived women's movement, flourished.

The Psychedelic Revival

Now, psychedelics are back again. But this time, there's a difference:

• While government policies remain conservative, there's a more liberal attitude about drugs among many people. Indeed, now there seems to be two radically different cultures: those who've tried drugs and those who haven't. And the number of people experimenting with drugs continues to grow.

• Recreational use, especially among people under 30, is more cutting edge as new designer drugs synthesized in the laboratory have proliferated.

• A recent Columbia University study showed that marijuana consumption has doubled among teenagers. Likewise, the University of Michigan, which has been tracking trends in drug usage, finds it has increased, particularly among high school and college kids.

Perhaps the most overt example of the psychedelic revival can be found at "raves." High-tech, high-decibel, computer-generated music, psychedelic drugs, and marathon dancing swirl continuously for as much as three to four days. On a typical weekend in the San Francisco Bay area, there may be 20,000 to 30,000 teenagers dancing around the clock, 80 percent of them under the influence of drugs.

Another sign of the times is a surge in use of MDMA, a

laboratory-synthesized variant of a hallucinogen that naturally occurs in the body. It's the new drug of choice among those who formerly ingested LSD, and went on to pursue chemical-free spiritual awareness. Also known as Ecstasy, it's a cross between a psychedelic and an amphetamine; in the majority of users it creates a sense of loving presence and an improved reorientation toward intimate relationships. And it deepens meditative calmness.

A 1987 survey of Stanford University students showed that 39 percent had taken MDMA at least once. By the end of the 1980s, an estimated 10,000 doses per month were in circulation in the U.S.; by 1993, six million doses a year were manufactured in home-based laboratories.

Even though the Drug Enforcement Administration classified MDMA as a substance with no medical use and high abuse potential in 1986, scientific research is still permitted by the government. But it's been limited almost exclusively to animal studies, according to the California Society of Addiction Medicine.

Meanwhile, drug use has become so sophisticated that it has spawned one of the hot new topics on the Internet—ethnobotany, the study of sacred plants in non-technological cultures. As fast as experts identify psychedelic plant substances used in native religious ceremonies around the world, youthful entrepreneurs with Ph.D.'s in chemistry trade their formulas on the Internet. Cyberspace is abuzz with recipes for psychedelic chemicals so new they're not yet even classed as illegal.

Dangers of Recreational Use

There can be no doubt, however, that in the history of psychedelic drug use, lives have been lost, and minds permanently altered. Sometimes people who smoke marijuana become disoriented and confused, rather than calm and enlightened. Intrepid mushroom gatherers have been known to ingest fungi that only looked similar to psilocybin—and died shortly thereafter. People have taken LSD and committed suicide.

In addition, animal studies show that neurological damage occurs when extremely large doses of psychedelics are ingested. Though comparable human damage has not been conclusively established, it's now well known that attitude, environment, and drug purity often influence how they affect us. In general, psychedelics are a poor choice for people barely able to keep their daily lives together, or those who live marginally. Borderline psychotics, people with a predisposition to mental illness, those with severe compulsions, or those with a tendency to abuse other substances, like alcohol, often don't do well when they ingest psychedelics purely for recreational purposes.

Physician-Supervised Use

At the same time recreational use is increasing, a host of psychiatric and medical benefits from physician-supervised use of psychedelic compounds is emerging.

• *LSD-assisted psychotherapy.* Researchers are exploring the use of LSD to accelerate the process of psychotherapy in the treatment of persistent problems such as personality disorder, obsessive compulsive behavior, and depression. Some psychiatrists believe that under the properly guided influence of these drugs, personal identity can be more easily restructured, compulsions based on subconscious ideas more easily rooted out, and that depression is countered by elevated mood states that persist after the physiological effects have abated.

For example, in the early 1970s, the Maryland Psychiatric Research Clinic applied psychedelics to the treatment of chronic alcoholism. It achieved a reported recovery rate of 50 percent.

More recently, between 1988 and 1993, the Swiss government licensed a group of psychiatrists, all members of the Swiss Medical Society for Psycholytic Therapy (psycholytic refers to the administration of psychedelics in relatively low doses), to begin LSD-assisted psychotherapy with patients who hadn't improved after standard psychiatric treatment. All of the patients had been diagnosed with conditions ranging from personality disorder to affective disorder and adjustment problems. By the end of treatment, 90 percent reported slight to good improvement. Nevertheless, due to mounting pressure from other governments, the Swiss ended the therapy.

Today [in 1996], prospects for research into LSD therapy in the U.S. remain uncertain. So far, the Food and Drug Administration (FDA) has approved only one scientific study of LSD—but it has floundered for lack of adequate funding. No public organization will finance such research. Some private funding has been available, but the amounts are meager.

Studies with Other Hallucinogens

• *Ibogaine.* This plant substance from West Africa, used in Gabon puberty rites, is being investigated for treatment of cocaine and heroin addiction. Tried on a group of heroin addicts in 1962, the drug was found to extinguish the craving associated with withdrawal. One of those successfully cured, Howard Lotsof, crusaded for its use and in the mid-80s convinced a Belgian company to manufacture it for distribution to addicts in the Netherlands, where drug policies are more lenient than the U.S. Although it proved moderately successful when tested on a group of 60 subjects, psychiatrist Herbert Kleber, M.D., director of the division of substance abuse at Columbia University College of Physicians and Surgeons in New York, remains cautious. "The evidence is anecdotal and not based on careful scientific studies," he says.

Nevertheless, medical science is seeking a cure for heroin and cocaine addiction and ibogaine looks like a possibility. "Right now we have no other drug that looks as good," confirms Curtis Wright, M.D., a medical officer of the FDA, which recently approved limited trials for ibogaine on cocaine addicts at the University of Miami.

• *MDMA.* In 1994, the FDA also approved studies to establish MDMA's safety. Psychiatrist Charles Grob, M.D., of UCLA, plans to test it in the relief of physical pain and psychological trauma in end-stage cancer patients, in treating post-traumatic stress disorder among veterans, and in the relief of chronic back and arthritis pain. Its effect on brain chemistry is also under study.[1]

• *Psilocybin.* Since 1990, the National Institute of Drug Abuse has funded Richard Strassman, M.D., associate professor of psychiatry at the University of New Mexico, to study the potential uses of psilocybin, the psychedelic derived from mushrooms. He's investigating its use in the treatment of schizophrenia and as an adjunct to psychotherapy.

• *Marijuana.* Its active ingredient, THC, or tetrahydracannabinol, helps relieve pain among cancer patients and eases nausea and gastrointestinal problems in HIV-positive and AIDS patients. Despite the fact that no one else can legally use it, in the 1970s the FDA initiated an extremely limited program to distribute marijuana to people with glaucoma, chronic pain, and spasticity. By 1989, the program also included some AIDS patients. In 1992, the program was cancelled by the Bush administration; they didn't want to be seen as endorsing the drug.[2]

As of 1996, eight of the original recipients continue to receive the drug, which the government grows at the University of Mississippi.

When media attention increased applications to the program, federal authorities instead began to advocate using THC in pill form. According to FDA spokesman William Grigg, thousands of patients who receive chemotherapy benefit from the pills. But critics contend that it's easier to regulate the dosage when the drug is inhaled. In any case, according to a recent survey conducted by Harvard researchers, 44 percent of specialists said they told their patients to use marijuana to counter the nausea from chemotherapy, even though it's illegal. . . .

---

1. Grob later changed the focus of his study to psilocybin.   2. In the late 1990s, voters in California and Oregon voted to legalize medical marijuana. Although the Supreme Court barred the distribution of medical marijuana in 2000, some individuals have access to it through doctors' prescriptions.

Psychedelics and the Brain

Sparked partly by the recent discovery that the body makes its own opioids, an entirely new field of neurochemistry has sprung up that views the human body as a giant chemical factory.

For two thousand years science has focused its attention on the brain and the hard wiring of the nervous system as the seat of intelligence and consciousness. Now, however, brain cells have been found to secrete chemical messengers, called peptides, that allow the brain to communicate with individual cells floating through the body that are not in direct contact with any part of the central nervous system. Researchers at MIT dubbed this new information loop the "parasynaptic information network" and postulated that it may be the main avenue by which information is exchanged between the mind and body.

Georgetown professor Candice Pert, Ph.D., has taken this hypothesis one step further and proposed that the type of information exchange going on in this network is related to mood as well as autonomic functioning. Peptides may hold the key to the biochemistry of the emotions. If the brain is aware of and in communication with individual cells in the body, peptides may be the key to the biology of consciousness.

Consequently, the race is on to draw the precise chemical map of brain sites where different substances bind with target cells through complex lock-and-key mechanisms called receptors. One of the newest discoveries is that the body appears to produce not only its own opioid-like compounds, but its own psychedelic-like compounds as well.

Scarcely a week goes by that new substances are not being discovered and reported in neuroscience literature. One of the most recent findings is that marijuana, instead of interrupting brain processes the way other drugs do, stimulates in the brain specific receptors normally meant to receive the body's own psychedelic compounds. Substances like marijuana have their effect on us because they accidentally fit these inborn receptors so well.

In 1988 researchers discovered the brain receptor that

binds with the THC molecule. The conclusion was inescapable—there must therefore be natural THC-like brain molecules that trigger this same receptor. In 1992, researchers at the Hebrew University in Jerusalem discovered it was arachadonic acid, a substance common to all cells. Because of the euphoric effects of THC they called it anandamide (ananda means bliss in Sanskrit). These investigators then went on to confirm anandamide's cannabinoid properties. (When tested in mice, it created a spasm in the sex organs, as THC does.)

Exactly what do anandamide-making chemicals do in the nervous system? Researchers are now trolling for possibly overlooked cannabinoids in the brain—and searching for synthetic drugs that have the same effects as marijuana. The yield may be new medicines that act as painkillers and antihypertensives, as well as compounds that prevent nausea and lower eye pressure in glaucoma.

The Big Picture

Looking at the big picture, there are two revolutions in process: one in the lab, designed to unlock the chemical complexities of consciousness, the other in popular culture, focused on the spiritual evolution of personality. Because psychedelics are playing a key role in each, these two cultural forces are destined to meet. What part psychedelics will play, however, is still uncertain. As Lester Grinspoon, M.D., the distinguished Harvard psychiatrist, has said, "Psychedelics are truly a double-edged sword. On the one hand, they have potential for harm, on the other, tremendous potential for good. How to minimize the harm so it is overshadowed by the good remains the central question to be answered."

The Toxic Legacy of Timothy Leary

Roger Kimball

Roger Kimball is the managing editor of the monthly journal *New Criterion* and an art critic for the London *Spectator*. He is also the author of several books on culture, history, and politics, including *The Long March: How the Cultural Revolution of the 1960s Changed America*. In the following essay, Kimball examines the influence of 1960s countercultural figure Timothy Leary, the Harvard psychologist who experimented with hallucinogenic drugs and advocated their use. In Kimball's opinion, Leary was a profoundly irresponsible researcher who made outlandish claims about the effects of hallucinogens. Although his allegations were obviously misguided, Leary's influence has undermined American moral values, writes Kimball. Even after the heyday of psychedelic drugs, American culture is dominated by the desire for rule breaking, unlimited ecstasy, and unearned transcendence.

> For us the planet was without Original Sin, designed for our sacramental pleasure.
> —Timothy Leary, *Flashbacks: An Autobiography*

No account of America's cultural revolution can omit the career of Timothy Leary, "promoter, apologist, and high priest of psychedelia nonpareil," as Theodore Roszak put it in *The Making of a Counterculture* (1969). Dr. Timothy Leary, Ph.D., had his first experience of LSD in the spring of 1962 when he was forty-two and teaching in the psychology department at Har-

Roger Kimball, "The Project of Rejuvenilization," *New Criterion*, vol. 16, May 1998, p. 4. Copyright © 1998 by the Foundation for Cultural Review. Reproduced by permission of the author.

vard University. In the summer of 1963, Leary and his colleague Richard Alpert—who would later turn himself into a
guru and take the Hindu name Baba Ram Dass—would be expelled from the Harvard faculty for disseminating drugs to students. But in the meantime they were sedulous in "researching" the effects of these drugs. For the previous two years,
Leary and Alpert had eagerly "experimented"—to use the preferred euphemism—both on themselves and on hundreds of
others with various hallucinogenic drugs, especially psilocybin. But LSD was something new and much more powerful. It
had, Leary knew, been secretly tested by the CIA in the late
1950s for possible use in interrogations and unconventional
warfare. In the words of an official intelligence document, LSD
was "capable of rendering whole groups of people, including
military forces, indifferent to their surroundings and situations, interfering with planning and judgment, and even creating apprehension, uncontrollable confusion and terror."

Leary's introduction to the drug came through an English
academic named Michael Hollingshead. "On the basis of his
claim to have ingested more LSD than anyone in the world,"
Leary recalled in *Flashbacks*, the autobiography he published in
1983, "I invited him to stay at our house and act as a project
consultant." A short while before, Hollingshead had inadver-
tently taken a large dose of LSD with a colleague. "They became," Leary wrote, "mystics on the spot."

The Disciple of Hallucinogens

Like so many apostles of mind-altering drugs, Timothy Leary
was very big on the idea of becoming a mystic on the spot. He
did it hundreds, indeed thousands, of times. Leary first sampled hallucinogenic drugs in Mexico in 1960 (more "research"
for his new job at Harvard). Describing the experience years
later, he wrote that

> I gave way to delight, as mystics have for centuries when they
> peek through the curtains and discovered that this world—so

manifestly real—was actually a tiny stage set constructed by the mind. . . .

Starting back to the terrace. Hello, my walk had changed to a rubber-leg slither. The room was apparently filled with invisible liquid. I undulated over to Poet Betty. Her classic face unfolded like a sunflower. She was in some sort of bliss. . . .

Next came a trip through evolution, guaranteed to everyone who signs up to this Brain Tour. Slipping down the recapitulation tube to those ancient mid-brain projection rooms: snake-time, fish-time, down-through-giant-jungle-palm-tree-time, green lacy fern leaftime. . . . Hello, I am the first living thing.

The journey lasted a little over four hours. Like almost everyone who has had the veil drawn, I came back a changed man.

Among other things, he discovered that "the world was divided into those who had had the experience (or were eager to have it) and those who had not (and shuddered at the possibility)."

Preposterous Claims

Such pronouncements are a wearying staple of Leary's many books and pamphlets about the "mind-expanding" properties of hallucinogens. *The Psychedelic Experience* (1964), *Psychedelic Prayers from the Tao Te Ching* (1967), *How to Start Your Own Religion* (1967), *The Politics of Ecstasy* (1968), *High Priest* (1968), and on and on. They all revolve around Leary's reports of the life-changing enlightenment that he enjoyed thanks to drugs. When he was finally introduced to LSD, he found it "the most shattering experience of my life."

I have never recovered from that ontological confrontation. I have never been able to take myself, my mind, or the social world quite so seriously. Since that time, I have been acutely aware that everything I perceive, everything within and around me, is a creation of my own consciousness. And that everyone lives in a neural cocoon of private reality. From that day I have never lost the sense that I am an actor, surrounded by characters, props, and sets for the comic drama being written in my brain.

Untangling everything that is incoherent and preposterous about such reports would require many pages. Just for starters, one might ask why, if everyone is trapped in the cocoon of a private reality, anyone bothers to write books advertising the fact. Who could read them? And if Leary's amateur solipsism were right, how could such a thing as a book even exist? Think about how much solid social reality there must be before books could be written, printed, circulated, read. And on the question of mystical illumination, what depths of credulity must be plumbed before someone could mistake a deliberate pharmacological assault on the nervous system for an experience of divine truth, a chemical emergency for an "ontological confrontation"? Among other things, such credulity reminds one of how elaborate are the excuses one can generate and embrace for the sake of a hedonistic evasion of reality. Leary's perception that he had become an actor in a comic drama of his own making has a little more to be said for it, though it would be more accurate to describe the situation he created as a tragedy with distinctly farcical elements. In any event, histrionics, not to say melodrama—not to say outright hucksterism—played a prominent part in Leary's activities from the beginning.

A Pathetic Figure

Long before his death in 1996 at the age of seventy-six, Timothy Leary had become an absurd, indeed a pathetic, figure. The absurdity and the pathos culminated in the gruesome theater of his death. Leary directed that his brain be cryogenically preserved "with the expectation of reanimation and brain-transplant to a healthy body in the future." ("It seems to me" he explained, "that the person who dies a 'natural' death is a deluded victim of state-managed suicide.") His final moments and the surgical removal of his head were captured on video tape for the edification of his acolytes.

Leary's preposterousness did not make his influence any less widespread or any less malign. His life was in many respects a cautionary tale—not least as an example of the extent to which it had become possible to be ridiculous and profoundly destructive at the same time. This in fact was an amalgam that the Sixties rather specialized in. Like many of his peers, Leary illustrated the fact that being an object of pity does not necessarily exempt someone from being also an object of censure.

Phony Spirituality

His advocacy of hallucinogens was, as Theodore Roszak put it, the advocacy of a "counterfeit infinity." Roszak was himself an apologist for many aspects of the counterculture. But like many politically committed Leftists, he understood that Leary's obsession with drugs was not aiding the cause of political revolution and that his assurance that "the LSD trip is a religious pilgrimage" was a gross, psychically maiming deception—of himself, possibly; certainly of the thousands upon thousands whom he seduced with his gospel of instant ecstasy. Leary produced an endless stream of books, pamphlets, and manifestos (his annotated bibliography runs to 305 pages). But his teaching—if "teaching" is the word—is accurately epitomized in his most famous slogan: "Turn on, tune in, drop out," a pithy formula he came up with in 1966 after Marshall McLuhan (himself a false prophet of considerable influence) advised him that "your advertising must stress the religious."

Three decades on, it is difficult to recapture the peculiar intensity of Leary's presence in the 1960s and early 1970s. A popular rock band, The Moody Blues, wrote a hit song about him; he fraternized with the superchic from New York to Hollywood and San Francisco; in 1970, when he planned to run for Governor of California, John Lennon of The Beatles wrote a campaign song for him; President [Richard] Nixon described him as "the most dangerous man in America." For a brief period in the mid- to late Sixties, Leary was ubiquitous: a beaming, gurulike presence at the first Love-Ins and Be-Ins, barefoot and ponytailed, dressed in white duck trousers and flowing white silk shirt, spouting such nostrums as "Laws are made by old people who don't want young people to do exactly those things young people were meant to do—to make love, turn on, and have a good time.". . .

Researcher, Hedonist, and Martyr

It is worth noting that Leary the "researcher" was never content simply to dispense drugs to others and record their reactions; right from the beginning, he was a participant, eagerly seizing every opportunity for intoxication, even when he experimented with psilocybin on prisoners in the Concord State Prison. ("The bowl of pills was placed in the center of the table. To establish trust I was the first to ingest.") It should be noted, too, that Leary got his wish: it really was only a year or two before college students became quite expert at "activating their own nervous systems" with drugs. There was nothing to it, really. The manufacturers didn't need to supply elaborate "instructions."

If Leary brought the authority of Harvard and the Ivy League to the counterculture, he brought it as a chastened, a dethroned authority. That is part of what made him so seductive. Leary was a Harvard professor who had seen through the "superficialities" and conventions of the hidebound academic establishment:

> I was at that time a successful robot—respected at Harvard, clean-cut, witty, and, in that inert culture, unusually creative. Though I had attained the highest ambition of the young American intellectual, I was totally cut off from body and senses. My clothes had been obediently selected to fit the young professional image. Even after one hundred drug sessions I routinely listened to pop music, drank martinis, ate what was put before me.

Leave aside the sillinesses in this passage. The important

thing is that Leary had discovered how to have the best of both worlds. He could enjoy the prestige of being a Harvard professor and the delicious frisson of rejecting it all at the same time. His expulsion from Harvard further burnished his image: now he was a martyr as well as a witness for a truth too dangerous for "the establishment" to accommodate. . . .

Leary's Damaging Influence

It is easy to dismiss Timothy Leary as a misguided crank, a period figure whose relevance disappeared with bell-bottoms and love beads. This would be a mistake. Leary was undoubtedly a crank, and he was assuredly profoundly misguided. But his example was immensely influential. His importance extends far beyond the thousands of lives he blighted with drugs. As much as anyone, he helped to change the moral temper of the times. Long after taking psychedelics ceased to be a preferred recreational pastime, the rationale that Leary provided for indulging in such drugs retained a large measure of credibility: they "increased sensitivity," even "increased intelligence," they freed one from "conventions" and produced "mystical" feelings of unbounded ecstasy. "With the aid of these drugs," Leary wrote, "I was exposing myself to the most intense emotions available to the human nervous system." In fact, he was exposing himself to a seductive counterfeit of emotion: a spiritual, soul-withering lie in capsule form. In "The Legacy of the Late Sixties," the philosopher Harvey Mansfield observes that the phrase "mind-expanding" as applied to drugs is intended to mean

> something grander than merely opening a mind previously closed by prejudice or superstition. It means actually expanding what the mind can grasp and conveys the excitement . . . [of] freeing oneself not only from conventions but even from one's nature. Man is an animal that naturally lives by conventions, so denying his conventions is denying his nature and replacing it with the desire to go beyond whatever has been fixed, crossing all boundaries, breaking all rules. The appeal of drugs is that of infinite power together with infinite de-

sire. No doubt there is in human nature a yearning to rise above conventions, on occasion to get high. Previously this was thought necessary to control; now it was let loose among the young of the elite and invested with the moral superiority that comes from knowing that the system was corrupt.

A Permanent Holiday from Virtue

Leary and his fellow champions of chemical emancipation helped to acclimatize our entire culture to a demand for blind emotional transport: a feeling of illumination vouchsafed by darkness. Drugs opened up one road to this goal; rock music, as Leary understood, opened up another. Allan Bloom was quite right when he noted, in *The Closing of the American Mind*, that "rock music provides premature ecstasy and, in this respect, is like the drugs with which it is allied. It artificially produces the exaltation naturally attached to the completion of the greatest endeavors—victory in a just war, consummated love, artistic creation, religious devotion, and discovery of the truth." It was hardly surprising that Bloom's attack on rock music was one of the most widely castigated sections of his book. Writing in the mid-1980s, Leary reported that some 80 percent of the American public was "currently involved in personal fulfillment projects, most of which involve some form of rejuvenilization." No doubt he was right. And that, finally, is what Timothy Leary was all about: rejuvenilization. What he offered was not greater intelligence, feeling, and sophistication, but a permanent holiday from those virtues for the sake of a delusion as toxic as it is widely embraced.

Peyote Use by Native Americans Is Legitimate

Mike Kiyaani and Thomas J. Csordas

In the following selection Navajo healer Mike Kiyaani discusses his introduction to the medicinal use of the hallucinogenic peyote cactus; he also describes a typical peyote ceremony, in which he and a patient both ingest peyote to address the patient's illness or spiritual problem. As writer and anthropologist Thomas J. Csordas notes, the Navajo first encountered peyote through the practices of the Native American Church in the 1930s. The Navajo tribal government initially criminalized the peyote cult, not accepting it as an alternative ceremonial practice until 1966. Furthermore, the U.S. government did not fully legalize the ritual use of peyote among Native Americans until 1994. Kiyaani maintains that peyote enables humble Indian seekers to identify their sickness, which leads to healing—but he disapproves of its use among white people, who he believes are less sincere.

Thomas J. Csordas: Most Americans know peyote only as a cactus containing an illegal psychotropic substance, but to some 250,000 American Indian adherents of the peyote religion, it is a sacrament and a spirit. To live according to its inspiration is to follow the peyote road of personal dignity and respect for nature and for other people. Those recognized as having the ability to lead others along this path are known as "road men." Mike Kiyaani, who underwent his own long apprenticeship, is such a road man. Now seventy-seven, Kiyaani is a Navajo who first used peyote in the late 1940s, after returning to his native Arizona as an honored veteran of military service. He had served in an elite Marine unit, along with other Navajos who used their complex native language to communicate sensitive information—a code that defied penetration.

The Native American Church

The peyote religion, formally institutionalized as the Native American Church, was introduced to the Navajos in the 1930s by members of several Plains Indian tribes. Its practices and spirituality differ from those of the traditional Navajo religion, although both are fundamentally concerned with healing. Traditional Navajo medicine men—Kiyaani's own father was one—lead ceremonies known as chants. Lasting as long as nine consecutive nights, chants involve prayers in the form of songs, specific acts by the healer and patient, and the creation of potent visual symbols such as sand paintings. A peyote ceremony, in contrast, is a prayer meeting during which peyote is eaten by participants under the leadership of a road man. Combining singing, drumming, and prayers, the ceremony typically lasts one night, from dusk to dawn.

Assembled in a tepee or hogan, the participants focus their prayers on an altar or fire place. In the style learned by Mike Kiyaani, the centerpiece of the fire place is a crescent of heaped-up earth on which rests a special cactus button known as the chief peyote. The road man cherishes his chief peyote and may pass it down through several generations. Kiyaani concentrates on his chief peyote and the fire place to facilitate his dialogue with nature. He says that whereas white people talk directly to God, the humble prefer going through the intermediary of nature—the air and the sunshine, which are God's creations. Kiyaani is not a shaman who takes spirit flights to other worlds but a healer who prays through the elements of nature in which, for him, God already resides.

Mike Kiyaani's mentor was Truman Dailey, an Oto Indian who instructed him not to imitate Plains Indian ways but to take the medicine home and adapt its use to the Navajo culture and way of life. For Dailey, the elements of the altar represent parts of the eagle, which is sacred to his clan. Kiyaani stresses the Navajo understanding of corn as a symbol of growth and life. He performs the traditional corn pollen blessing, sprinkling some grains to make a path that corresponds to the peyote road. He also uses a song learned from his father that metaphorically connects the prayer meeting to the growth of the life-giving corn plant.

Navajo adherents of the peyote religion once faced opposition from their own tribal government, which decreed the religion illegal in 1940 and did not move for tolerance until 1966. Only in 1994 did the federal government adopt a law that guarantees the right of American Indians to practice the peyote religion. Mike Kiyaani remains deeply concerned that, against the background of a long struggle for freedom of religion, the use of peyote be protected for its importance in healing, spirituality, and identity. He has traveled widely to describe his work to audiences of health care professionals, and on the reservation his reputation as a road man keeps him in great demand by Navajos who travel considerable distances to seek his assistance.

Taking the Medicine

Mike Kiyaani: I'm a Navajo veteran—World War II, Navajo Code Talker, wounded in action. My clan is Salt Clan. I got my name from Kiyaani; that's my grandfather's clan. When I came back from the war, I was a sick man. There was something wrong with my mind, something wrong all over my body. No pain, but I felt kind of lousy. My father had died in 1944, and I guess that's what got into me. One man I got acquainted with took me to Oklahoma. I met this man Truman Dailey there, and he noticed my condition. He said, "You take this peyote," and gave me a twenty-five-pound flour sack filled with Mexican dry peyote. I took that back home.

During that time I was way up there where nobody lives, herding sheep, and I used peyote. Just a little bit during the day, every day. It seemed like it went all through my system. Then one particular day I felt like eating, and I had fifty buttons. In about another hour and a half, I ate another fifty buttons—maybe four times, fifty buttons. At midnight everything started

 THE HISTORY OF DRUGS

A Song of the Children of Peyote

What pretty hills, what pretty hills,
So very green where we are.
Now I don't even feel,
Now I don't even feel,
Now I don't even feel like going to my rancho . . .

Amid the flowers (peyote), so pretty.
Nothing but flowers here,
Pretty flowers, with brilliant colors,
So pretty, so pretty,
And eating one's fill of everything,
Everyone so full here, so full with food.
The hills very pretty for walking . . .

For we are all,
We are all,
We are all the children of,
We are all the sons of
A brilliantly colored flower,
A flaming flower.
And there is no one,
There is no one,
Who regrets what we are.

Huichol peyote seekers, quoted in Peter T. Furst, *Hallucinogens and Culture*, 1976.

coming. My life seemed to be coming to an end. That's the way the medicine showed me, but I still kept on eating until morning. Everything began coming out different. There was a lot of sagebrush out there, and everything was too beautiful. But every time I looked to the peyote, it wasn't pleasant to look at.

Then toward noon I looked for that peyote, and now I saw it was real pure, real white. It kind of talked to me, "Your body is like that, your body is pure. Now you don't need treatment, you're a well man. You wanted to get well, now you're well." I understood it to be that way. At that time I sure cried. I was all right then. After that I was pretty much on the go most of the time performing ceremonies for sick people. I kind of experimented with the peyote eating, how it works, how it can heal.

The Peyote Ceremony

At the start of the ceremony, I don't know what's ailing the patient, but when you take some peyote into your system, the peyote affects you, and then you kind of know. A lot of people just say, "I'm sick," that's all. They don't know exactly what's bothering them. But peyote does wonderful things. My patient eats peyote. He has peyote in his system. Peyote is in my system, too. He's talking; then I kind of know. I kind of see things, what's wrong in that way. It's the peyote that shows me things. It's my patient talking his mind—the way he talks, the way he expresses himself. It might be his action in there that's kind of unusual; that tells me. But I don't watch him directly, I keep my eyes on the fire all the time.

I say, "You come to me, and I want you to help yourself; whatever it is that's bothering your mind, whatever it is you think that's bothering your health, get your mind off of it. You get on to this medicine, this fire place, this singing that you hear, the prayers that you are hearing in here, which are all for you. The people sitting here, they're talking for you. They're singing for you. Everybody wants you to get well. Whatever's bothering you—maybe it's an evil, maybe it's that lightning struck near you, maybe something else. Get your mind off of it." He might have a hard time [from nausea] through the peyote effect, but that's going to help him. That's the time he's going to figure out what's wrong, why he's sick.

I go outside for a special ceremony at midnight. I get my bone whistle out. Some medicine men take their flashlight out there or maybe take somebody with them out there. I don't do those things. I'd rather be in the dark, praying by myself. A lot of Navajos, while they're out there, they see something, visualize something. I don't look for those things. But I might be hearing that the patient's mind is bothered by witchcraft or maybe some lightning struck that might be affecting his body, his mind.

Talking with Nature

Peyote. You eat it and it goes through your body, your blood veins, your flesh, your bone, your brain, and we talk to this peyote. And this peyote goes through all the patient's blood veins, goes to his brain, brain vessel; it seems like we talk to the peyote like that. Talking with nature; that's all it is. Whatever you do, peyote knows it, nature knows it. Whatever is wrong inside here, nature knows it. The Almighty knows it, so there's no way you can get away from this peyote, from this Almighty, from nature. If at some place you get off the road, then you notice it. Then you come back and pray. You go back to the Almighty, back to peyote. You get back on the road.

The spirit peyote came up among the Navajo people on a very hard road. But peyote found its way here, and so you see it has some kind of power. It found its way into the Navajo people, into the Navajo hogan, into the heart. Where the heart is, this peyote goes in there. So I want this thing to go on, this peyote religion, peyote worship. It's something for Indians who are humble. Just like in the Bible—it says the meek shall inherit the earth.

Now I'm worried the white man is going to go for it. That's

what they usually do. That's what we don't want to happen. I don't think it's for the white people. This natural herb peyote is used by Native Americans with more sincerity. Indian people are more serious in their mind, in their heart, in the way they worship. Just let the Indians have it, let the Indians use it the way they want it, just natural. Our identity is there.

PCP Has Reemerged as a Serious Problem

Timothy W. Maier

Phencyclidine (PCP), a hallucinogenic drug that was initially sold as a veterinary anesthetic, enjoyed some popularity from the 1960s through the 1980s, writes Timothy W. Maier in the following article. PCP was known for causing bizarre hallucinations and "bad trips" as well as loss of physical coordination, convulsions, violent behavior, and terrifying flashbacks. Although PCP seemed to disappear in the 1990s, it is currently experiencing a comeback, particularly among teens attending all-night rave parties. Authorities are especially concerned because drugs sold as Ecstasy, a rave favorite, often contain traces of PCP. Maier contends that PCP has become popular again because it is cheap and because the media and the public have failed to take its dangers seriously. Maier is an investigative reporter.

Nearly two decades ago a Baltimore father on Christmas Eve experienced a bizarre hallucination as he gazed into the eyes of his year-old son. What the father saw terrified him. He told police that shortly after he had smoked PCP, he became convinced the boy was possessed by Satan. He grabbed a knife and cut off his son's head. Other such horrors began to surface in the 1980s when a killer was under the influence of PCP, or phencyclidine, a mind-altering drug.

"But that was the worst drug case I ever saw," recalls

Michael M. Gimbel, director of the Baltimore County Department of Health's Bureau of Substance Abuse. "It's been stuck in my head for 20 years." Gimbel was greatly relieved in the 1990s when PCP all but disappeared. It had delivered so many "bad trips" that it drove its users nearly into extinction, he says. Side effects included some lasting health problems such as respiratory difficulties, slurred speech, severe agitation, flashbacks, hallucinations, lost coordination and convulsions. In some cases, PCP sent users into terrifying flashbacks or hallucinations long after even a first smoking, snorting or swallowing of the drug.

PCP first made its appearance in the 1950s as an anesthetic for medical procedures, but it didn't last long. So many patients experienced such severe confusion and delirium that its development for human use was discontinued. In the 1960s, it became commercially available as a veterinary anesthetic under the trade name Sernylan. It burst into the counterculture in 1967 during the heyday of the Haight-Ashbury district in San Francisco when it was sprayed onto cigarettes or marijuana. Black-market dealers called it the "Peace Pill," but users soon learned it was anything but peaceful. In 1978, due to widespread abuse of Sernylan, it was discontinued even as a veterinary anesthetic.

The Return of PCP

Incredibly, today PCP is back, bringing with it a torrent of violence and filling courtrooms with horror stories. In Washington alone there were 203 crime-related PCP cases in 2002 compared to just 31 in 1999. Nationwide, there were more than 6,000 PCP-related emergency-room visits in 2001 compared to about half that number in 1996.

"For some reason, people really fall in love with the drug," Gimbel says. "They like the feeling. It makes them feel godlike. But there's a saying on the street that sums up the drug: 'PCP will put a horse on its ass. Imagine what it will do to you.'"

"Michael," a former PCP user and dealer, calls it a drug for people who want to escape reality. "It has an all-numbing feeling.". . ."You can punch your hand through a window and you feel no pain. But you feel so awful when coming off of it that you are inclined to do more. It's not a high, it makes you forget so you don't have to deal with issues. It's a big forget-me pill."

According to Michael, he started smoking PCP at age 17 in the mid-1980s and stopped five years later when he landed in prison on robbery and murder charges, although he says PCP was obtained easily by inmates. Peer pressure led him down the PCP path, he says. "All the kids were smoking it in high school, particularly girls. They really love this drug."

Some called it the "love boat" or "buck naked" because users tend to strip their clothes off while under the influence. Others called it "angel dust," "supergrass," "killer weed," "embalming fluid," and "rocket fuel." Today it is referred to as "dippers" because users dip a cigarette or marijuana joint into a PCP-laced liquid they call "water," says Washington-based private investigator Sharon Weidenfeld, who studies about 30 murder cases a year.

"I first noticed the comeback of PCP in 2000 when I investigated a murder case in Rockville, Md.," she says. "The victim was a heavy PCP user. He had just gotten a jar of [PCP-laced] water shortly before he was murdered. The victim and the people involved in smoking and selling PCP all lived about a mile away from the courthouse [in] one of the wealthiest counties in the country. Since then, PCP has played a part in most of the murder cases that I have worked on."

The Latest Rave Drug

However, PCP now is being trafficked differently and with a new urban myth. No longer is it confined to the metropolitan underbelly—it has become the latest club drug at suburban "rave" parties. "The comeback of PCP has given new meaning to the ad, 'Got Milk?'" Weidenfeld says. "When people smoke dippers, they often are unable to move. The common belief is that the user has only to drink some milk to become unstuck. A conscientious PCP smoker simply makes sure to have some milk on hand in case of an emergency."

The milk myth makes little sense but then neither do the PCP murders, Weidenfeld says. "The mentality of these killings is different from those that occurred as a result of using crack," she reports. "A lot of that [killing] was over who was going to be allowed to hustle and where they could do it. The PCP murders don't even have a motive much of the time, and they seldom seem to so much as trouble the killer. I had one case where the user killed his close friend, went and smoked some dippers, got a hooker and then called it a night."

What worries authorities is that teenagers attending rave parties may have no idea that they have been slipped a hit of PCP. Many have been led to believe they are taking a hit of ecstasy, another dangerous club drug, but in reality they have been given PCP. In fact, authorities are warning that frequently drugs sold as ecstasy now have traces of PCP.

The Beginning of a Long Nightmare

The re-emergence of the drug has sent chills through the law-enforcement community, especially in light of a recent Maryland case that police say may have been the single largest such bust in the United States, if not the world. The news barely hit the radar screen of a jaded public and appears to have been all but ignored by both major Washington dailies and local news bureaus. The *Baltimore Sun* was the only newspaper to report on the raid, and it was all but cursory.

The bust capped a two-month undercover operation involving the U.S. Drug Enforcement Administration, the U.S. Bureau of Alcohol, Tobacco and Firearms and the Baltimore City Police Firearms Apprehension Strike Team. Authorities fear this may be only the beginning of a long nightmare to come as production facilities that formerly provided the drug operated only on the West Coast. Phencyclidine production was believed to be centered in the greater Los Angeles metropolitan area and to be controlled by the Crips, a Los Angeles-based street gang. They allegedly distribute PCP to many cities in the United States using their cocaine network. But the recent East Coast PCP bust seems to center around a biker gang that police have yet publicly to identify.

Authorities discovered the huge PCP lab in Baltimore shortly after an undercover detective purchased PCP on a local street. They made one arrest, but more are pending. Police seized at least 30 gallons of PCP and the production lab found in a basement of a Baltimore home. The estimated street value of the drugs is between $50 million and $100 million. "It was one of the biggest PCP labs of its kind on the East Coast," said Edward T. Norris, then Baltimore Police Commissioner.

In addition to a south Baltimore motorcycle gang, police are investigating a Jessup, Md., business for providing chemicals to make PCP. But it is the biker gang that reportedly is responsible for distributing PCP throughout the Washington/Baltimore metropolitan area, police say. The Jessup business has been identified as Marlo Industries, which processes a series of cleaning chemicals and packages them there. The company's clients include the White House, the federal Bureau of Engraving and Printing, Amtrak, Andrews Air Force Base and both Baltimore and Philadelphia housing authorities. Owners of the company have declined to comment on the pending investigation.

The bust should have been a wake-up call to parents and a nation that believed PCP had been fought to a standstill. Even so, earlier signs appear to have been ignored. [In 2001], Fairfax County, Va., police encountered PCP-laced tablets during an undercover drug operation where traffickers were marketing it as a superpowerful drug that could be taken in pill form. But perhaps the scariest part of the latest bust involves the age of the customers the drug dealers were targeting. In an effort to attract younger children to the drug, small PCP tablets were embossed with a Pokemon cartoon character known as Pikachu. These confiscated PCP pills were orange in color and sold for $15 a piece.

An Acceptable Drug?

Why is PCP making a comeback? Some users claim it's because the drug is so cheap compared even to marijuana. Amazingly, it also might be more accepted. For example, when a prankster on the set of James Cameron's *Titanic* spiked the clam chowder with PCP, it was made out to be a joke. Former president Bill Clinton pardoned at least three big-time PCP dealers during his final days in office. And still there has been no public campaign to tackle this problem that has produced so many nightmares and unspeakable crimes.

A Case of Jimsonweed Psychosis

Pamela Grim

Pamela Grim is an emergency-room physician who lives in Cleveland, Ohio. She is also the author of *Just Trying to Save a Few Lives*, a collection of essays. In the following selection, Grim describes the treatment of a youth who was dropped off at an emergency room because he was suffering from a drug overdose. The youth had an abnormally high heart rate and was hallucinating and having seizures as a small team of doctors and nurses worked frantically to determine what drug he had taken. Eventually an intensive-care specialist discerned that the patient's hallucinations—leprechauns—revealed that he had been smoking jimsonweed.

I was writing up a chart when a message blared over the intercom: "There's a drive-by in the parking lot." A drive-by is a patient dropped off at the emergency room doorstep by someone making a quick getaway. A car slows. The driver pushes our next patient out and takes off in a cloud of exhaust and burning rubber. A drive-by can be a victim of anything: a drug overdose, gunshots, a stabbing, even a cardiac arrest.

I rounded up Matt Tang, a first-year resident, and Omar Veniciano, a nurse, and quickly headed for the parking lot. There we found a kid, no more than 18 or 19 years old, dressed only in underpants and wearing a leather hat with a feather in it. He looked around, confused and terrified, as we

---

Pamela Grim, "Runaway Heart," *Discover*, vol. 20, April 1999, p. 40. Copyright © 1999 by The Walt Disney Company. Reproduced by permission.

prepared to move him onto a gurney.

"Hey kid," I said. "What's your name?"

He mumbled a name that sounded like Raphael.

"Raphael, what happened?"

He grabbed my arm. "You've got to help me," he said. "The leprechauns are everywhere."

By the time we got Raphael to the ER and hooked him up to an IV and monitor, he was incoherent.

Detective Work

In emergency medicine, a case like this falls under the category Change in Mental Status of Unknown Etiology. The patient has no available history. The only clues come from the physical exam, laboratory tests, and the physician's best guesses. Given the mental challenge such cases present, it's not surprising that Arthur Conan Doyle, himself a physician, modeled Sherlock Holmes after a medical professor.

We usually begin the detective work by looking through the patient's clothes for a wallet or miscellaneous contents. In Raphael's case, we didn't have any pockets to turn out, so the resident and I started with the physical exam. Raphael's skin was red, but there was no sign of injury.

His lungs were clear, his belly soft. The most obvious abnormality was his pupils; they were so dilated that the irises had all but disappeared. He had the eyes of a cartoon character—two blank black saucers.

Raphael was muttering incessantly and began pushing us away. He scrambled off the end of the bed and then stopped. He just stood there, stark naked, looking around in fear and bewilderment.

"Security!" I shouted, reaching for the boy.

It took five of us to restrain him. We finally strapped him down and reattached him to the monitor. His heart rate was even faster than before—145 beats per minute and climbing. His skin was flushed.

I quizzed Matt: "Can you tell me the differential diagnosis in this case?"

"Encephalitis. (Inflammation of the brain.)

Drug overdose.

Intracranial bleeding. Hypoglycemia. Electrolyte abnormalities."

"Psychosis," Omar added.

Although anything on the list was possible, I had a strong suspicion Raphael was whacked out. But which drug? The most likely answer was cocaine, a lot of cocaine. Why else would someone with an overdose have a pulse this high?

The symptom profile of a patient with a drug overdose is called a toxidrome. A cocaine toxidrome includes a fast heart rate, high blood pressure, and profuse sweating.

But Raphael was dry as a bone. And the dilated pupils—you don't see that with a cocaine overdose.

There were, of course, other possibilities. Raphael could have been smoking PCP—an animal tranquilizer-cum-hallucinogen sold on the street. PCP can make you awfully confused and agitated, but it usually doesn't make your heart race.

"So what tests do you want to order?" I asked Matt.

"Glucose, chemistries, urine drug screen . . . ," he replied.

The urine drug screen would tell us whether Raphael had cocaine in his system, but the results wouldn't be available for an hour or two, at least.

A Climbing Heart Rate

Meanwhile, Raphael's heart rate kept climbing. It was now 158, and he was even redder than before and more agitated. He looked the way patients look just before they seize.

"I think we need to call for a pharmacological backup," I said. "Let's consult Seamus."

Seamus Herzog, an intensive-care specialist, had done a two-year toxicology fellowship. He had become our walking poison control center and a brilliant medical detective.

"Yo!" Seamus said when he answered his page. "I'll be down just like that!" In a few minutes he ambled into the ER, coffee cup in hand.

Matt presented the case. It was hard to concentrate as I watched Raphael's heart rate rising: 160 . . . 168. After the presentation, Seamus glanced over the patient, peeking into his eyes and tapping gently at his belly.

"This doesn't really sound like cocaine," he said. "Sounds like an anticholinergic overdose."

Anticholinergic overdose. A different toxidrome. Cocaine operates on the sympathetic nervous system, which mobilizes us for emergency action. An anticholinergic drug acts on the parasympathetic nervous system, which regulates activities when the body is at rest. The classic anticholinergic drug, atropine, is often used in the ER to treat a slow heart rate. The symptoms of an anticholinergic overdose include dry mouth, tachycardia, and fever. If the dose is high enough, the patient will also exhibit confusion. Other classes of drugs—antipsychotics, antidepressants, and even over-the-counter cold medications—can produce similar actions and symptoms. But I had never seen a patient with an anticholinergic overdose who was this sick.

"Do you know the nursery rhyme for the anticholinergic toxidrome?" Seamus asked Matt.

The resident looked startled. "What do you mean, nursery rhyme?"

"It lists the way patients present: red as a beet, blind as a bat, dry as a bone, mad as a hatter, hotter than hell."

We all looked down at Raphael. That description pretty much fit the way he looked.

Seizures

"What else do you see with anticholinergic overdoses?" Matt asked just as Raphael began seizing.

"Seizures," Seamus said, while Omar scrambled for some Valium.

We rolled Raphael over on his side and got the Ambu bag ready to give him oxygen.

"You'd have to take a lot of cold tablets to overdose this bad," I said.

"Maybe he took a lot of antipsychotics," Seamus said.

Omar gave Raphael the Valium. Nothing happened. He continued to seize. We gave him a little more Valium and still he seized.

"How about giving him some physostigmine?" Seamus said.

I shook my head. While physostigmine will block the effects of an anticholinergic drug, it has many side effects—bad side effects like seizures and slowed heart rate. The word itself made me shiver. It was not a drug to fool around with.

"What would happen with physostigmine?" the resident asked.

Seamus steepled his hands and peered over them wisely. "If this is an anticholinergic overdose, he'll stop seizing."

"And if it's cocaine?" I asked.

Seamus nodded. "He'll seize worse."

I gazed down at Raphael. His head was arched back, eyes twitching, froth on his lips. Maybe we were missing something big. Maybe this wasn't an overdose. But I felt in my bones that this was a kid looking to get high.

"We need to paralyze and intubate him," I told Omar, but as we pulled the intubation cart over and began to get ready, Raphael suddenly stopped seizing and lay still.

"Thank God," I said.

Lilliputian Syndrome

Seamus shook his head. "He's going to seize again."

"I don't want to give this kid physostigmine. It's a terrible drug."

Seamus looked down at Raphael. "Okay, let's start over. Tell me about it from the beginning."

I went back through the drop-off, the underwear, and the hat. "He said his name was Raphael, and that's about all. He was hallucinating."

"Did he say what he saw?"

"Well, it didn't make any sense, but he said he was seeing leprechauns everywhere."

Seamus grabbed my arm. "That's it!" he said. "That's the key! Lilliputian syndrome!"

"Lilliputian syndrome?"

"It's when you hallucinate and you see tiny . . . ," Seamus waved his hands, searching for the words, "tiny people. Lilliputians, like in Gulliver's Travels. There's only one drug that does that: stramonium, the psychoactive substance in jimsonweed."

"Jimsonweed," I repeated.

"What's jimsonweed?" the resident wanted to know.

"Jimsonweed is locoweed is Datura stramonium. The active ingredient is scopolamine, an alkaloid much like atropine. Same effect." Seamus raised his finger and assumed a teacher's pose. "The plant's name comes from the 1680s, when the English were invading America. Soldiers in Jamestown, Virginia, had a feast where they made a salad from a local plant, the datura plant. After they ate it, they hallucinated for hours and were completely, totally out of it. People called the plant Jamestown weed, and the name was eventually corrupted to jimsonweed. The stuff grows wild on the western plains. When cattle get into it, they pretty much look like the Jamestown soldiers must have looked. Plumb loco. Occasionally some idiot smokes it or eats it. Usually some stupid kid."

"Look! The patient's seizing again," the resident said.

We all looked down. I groaned.

Seamus put a hand on my arm. "What this kid needs is some physostigmine."

I shook my head. "Are you absolutely sure about this?"

He gave me a withering look. "Have I ever been wrong?"

A Good Sign

Okay, I thought to myself. I'm going to give someone physostigmine because he told me he saw leprechauns.

Omar drew up the drug and gave it. Then we all stood there helplessly watching Raphael seize.

It went on and on. I started racking my brains for other causes. Maybe the boy's problem was a ruptured blood vessel in the brain, or herpes encephalitis, or something else. Something that left a clue we somehow missed or misinterpreted.

Then, as suddenly as he started, Raphael lay still. Dead still.

"He's not breathing," Matt said. As I reached for the Ambu bag, Raphael turned his face to the side, gagged twice, catlike, and vomited vegetable matter all over the floor.

"No!" Seamus cried as I leaped forward. "That's a good sign."

Raphael sat up and looked around, dazed. "Who am I?"

"I was rather hoping you could tell us," I said.

Raphael kept looking around. "Wow, man, like everyone's looking at me. Hey, where's my hat? I think someone stole my hat."

Eventually Raphael confessed that he and two friends had smoked the seeds from several jimsonweed plants. They had heard somebody say it was just like marijuana.

"Well, looks like you heard wrong," Seamus told him.

Raphael hung his head.

I could see Matt wanted to ask Seamus something.

"I know about anticholinergic effects and all that," he said, "but can you tell me how you put all this together to figure it out?"

Seamus smiled at him. "It's very elementary," he said, patting the resident's back, "you just have to follow the clues."

Hallucinogens May Ease the Dying

Judith Lewis

Psilocybin, the psychoactive ingredient in hallucinogenic mushrooms, may reduce death anxiety in terminally ill patients, reports Judith Lewis in the following selection. Medical researcher Charles Grob, who is conducting a study to determine the effects of psilocybin on dying cancer patients, hopes to prove that the hallucinogen can significantly alter the experience of pain and reduce the emotional distress that accompanies impending death. Earlier studies with psilocybin suggested that the drug allows people to transcend the ego, an experience that may enable them to accept the loss of self that death entails. Although the federal government sometimes discourages such studies—fearing that they may undermine arguments against drug abuse—many researchers believe that they have an ethical responsibility to learn about the therapeutic potential of hallucinogens. Lewis is a journalist and features editor for *LA Weekly Times* magazine.

Almost as soon as Dr. Charles Grob secured approval to study the effects of psilocybin on Stage IV cancer patients, he faced another challenge, one nearly as formidable: recruiting 12 participants. Unlike so many other experiments in radical cancer treatment, Grob's does not offer a cure; he merely hopes to find that psilocybin, the most potent of the many compounds in psychedelic mushrooms, ameliorates a dying person's fear of death. The study targets patients relegated to 'palliative' treatment, people with metastatic cancer for whom there is no reasonable hope for remission. It is a segment of the population, says the National Cancer Policy Board of the Institute of Medicine—which put out a call in 2001 for 'novel' approaches to palliative treatment—largely ignored by medical science.

In this case, however, it has not been ignored by the Food and Drug Administration (FDA), which holds Grob's study to the same stringent requirements it applies to any study of any new drug. Participants in the study must have cancer of sufficient severity, but they must also be free of most other medical problems: high blood pressure, anemia, heart disease or liver dysfunction, brain tumors or metastases to the brain, kidney disease. In other words, says Grob's research nurse, Marycie Hagerty, "We're basically looking for healthy dying people."

Rigorous Criteria

Psilocybin is relatively safe—significantly safer, in fact, than the drug Grob had initially sought to use for the Study, MDMA (otherwise known as Ecstasy); according to most research, you'd have to ingest your own body weight in 'magic mushrooms' to poison yourself. But it's still a Schedule I drug, regarded by the federal authorities as having a high potential for abuse and no medical application. "I had to get the FDA, the DEA [Drug Enforcement Administration], the IRB [Institutional Review Board], the California Research Advisory Panel and our research committee here [at Harbor-UCLA] onboard," says Grob, who heads up the child-psychiatry division at Harbor-UCLA Medical Center. "Along the way, the criteria we had written initially got modified and tightened." For instance, where Grob and Hagerty had specified a systolic blood-pressure reading of 160 or lower, "after a great deal of discussion with the research committee here, we lowered it to 140. We're going to lose people with that."

According to Dr. Charles Schuster, a former director of the National Institute of Drug Abuse, now head of Wayne State

University's Substance Abuse Clinical Research Division, the federal government sometimes objects to such studies out of concern not only for the patients but for the overall mood of the country. "If psilocybin is shown to have some medical value," he says, "that might weaken the government's argument against it as a drug of abuse. I understand their concerns and share them, but if psilocybin or MDMA or any of these agents were to prove to have a unique therapeutic value for something we can't treat well currently, ethically we have a responsibility to pursue them." (Cocaine, he notes, is used in hundreds of thousands of nasal surgeries every year.)

Grob hopes to find that, in addition to reducing psychological distress associated with impending death, psilocybin is the rare substance that can safely reduce a cancer sufferer's need for pain medication—not because it blunts pain, as morphine does, but because it "changes one's perception of pain." He abandoned MDMA for mostly political reasons, after now-debunked research by George Ricaurte of Johns Hopkins University claimed one-time use of the drug could cause permanent brain damage. But he thinks psilocybin is better, anyway: "I was concerned about the possibility of cardiac arrhythmia associated with MDMA," he says. "And psilocybin might open up a deeper spiritual dimension for some people."

Transcending the Ego

In 1962, a physician and minister named Walter Pahnke conducted a double-blind study with 20 Protestant divinity students, who were administered capsules containing either 30 mg of psilocybin or a placebo just before Good Friday services at Boston's Marsh Chapel. Among them was the Rev. Mike Young, now a minister at the First Unitarian Church of Honolulu, who later reported having entered a mystical state in which he lost his fear of death. As he understands it now, the drug works because "human beings define their identities by this illusory thing called ego, which is constructed of memory and experience and determines who we think we are." In a controlled setting under the influence of psilocybin, "you transcend that ego. And to the person who no longer identifies with that 'who am I,' the loss of that self is no longer as threatening as it was before." The psilocybin trip was, Young recalls, "a pretty profound experience."

The 12 subjects ultimately recruited for Grob's study will be alternately administered psilocybin or a placebo in two separate sessions. The initial dose for the pilot study—which is primarily to establish the safety and efficacy of the drug in advance of a broader study sometime in the future—is 0.2 milligrams per kilogram of synthetic, single-alkaloid psilocybin, "the approved dose," says Grob. (A powerful mushroom experience would deliver about 0.3 milligrams of psilocybin per kilogram of body weight.) After each session, volunteers will be asked to evaluate their experience. Some of it may be unpleasant. "Hallucinogens uncover the truth," Grob says. "Sometimes the only way to get to the other side is to work through some of the darkness. They're going to have their hands held the whole time."

Previous Tests

Psilocybin has been tested in a clinical context before, most recently by Dr. Francisco Moreno at the University of Arizona, who is studying its effects on the symptoms of obsessive-compulsive disorder, and Franz X. Vollenweider, who completed a 'dose-effect' study [in 2003], establishing the drug's minimal risk to human health or psychological well-being. In the early 1960s, Stanislav Grof used another hallucinogen, DPT, along with LSD, to study existential anxiety in end-stage cancer patients; he found that the people he studied developed better attitudes about death, improved their relationships with family members and asked for less pain medication in the weeks and months following the experiment.

None of this figured into the Harbor-UCLA's Institutional

Review Board assessment of Grob's study, however when it sent back the first draft of its official patient-consent form, it read, "Benefits to Patient: None." Both Grob and Hagerty protested that there were indeed benefits, but they're hard to measure in medical terms. They also realize that the volunteer response might be small because most people with cancer aren't looking for a better way to die. They're looking for hope that they'll live.

Hagerty recalls a woman who responded shortly after she and Grob first sent out the call for recruits. "She was in her early 30s and had lung cancer. She had a little baby at home, and she was just desperate for anything that would help her live longer. She didn't know what psilocybin was, and I explained some of it to her and sent her to the Web site [www.canceranxietystudy.org] so she could read about it. Of course, I never heard back from her."

Another man called to refer his wife, who had already been assigned to palliative care but couldn't quite accept that she was dying. He told us, "She's not even thinking about death" says Hagerty. "She'll admit that she's Stage IV, but she doesn't think she's terminal. We heard that and changed the language, because how do you define 'terminal'? It's so variable, so negative. Medical science says to the 'terminal' patient, "Go off and take care of yourself; have a nice death." But a lot of people can live with Stage IV cancer for years.

Seeking Appropriate Candidates

Hagerty says that there has been no shortage of interest in the study, just not necessarily from appropriate candidates. "We're getting a lot of calls from people asking if we need any 'normal controls.' Meaning they'd be happy to take the psilocybin—they just don't happen to have cancer."

After two and a half months of putting out the call on e-mail lists and Web sites, Grob and Hagerty finally think they may have one participant: a man in New Mexico in the last stages of metastasized rectal cancer. "It's taken forever to get his lab work," says Grob, "because once his doctor had determined he couldn't be cured, his insurance wouldn't pay for new ones." Finally, his insurance provider complied, and he's just cleared a preliminary interview with George Greer of the Heffter Institute, the study's primary funder. "His red-blood-cell count was right on the border," says Grob. "But I got an okay from the people who run the research unit that it was good enough." He'd prefer that participants don't have to travel, "but at this point I can't be picky. I'm too anxious to get this study up and running."

How Drugs Are Classified

The Controlled Substances Act of 1970 classified drugs into five different lists, or schedules, in order of decreasing potential for abuse. The decision to place a drug on a particular schedule is based mainly on the effects the drug has on the body, mind, and behavior. However, other factors are also considered. The schedule is used to help establish the penalties for someone using or selling illegal drugs. On the other hand, sometimes a potentially valuable drug for treating a disease can be incorrectly scheduled, greatly hampering the exploration of its usefulness as a treatment.

Schedule of Controlled Substances

RATING	EXAMPLE
SCHEDULE I A high potential for abuse; no currently accepted medical use in the United States; or no accepted safety for use in treatment under medical supervision.	• Heroin • LSD • Marijuana • Mescaline • MDMA (Ecstasy) • PCP
SCHEDULE II A high potential for abuse; currently accepted medical use with severe restrictions; abuse of the substance may lead to severe psychological or physical dependence.	• Opium and Opiates • Demerol • Codeine • Percodan • Methamphetamines • Cocaine • Amphetamines
SCHEDULE III A potential for abuse less than the substances listed in Schedules I and II; currently accepted medical use in the United States; abuse may lead to moderate or low physical dependence or high psychological dependence.	• Anabolic steroids • Hydrocodone • Certain barbiturates • Hallucinogenic substances

Schedule of Controlled Substances

RATING	EXAMPLE
SCHEDULE IV A low potential for abuse relative to the substances listed in Schedule III; currently accepted medical use in the United States; limited physical or psychological dependence relative to the substances listed in Schedule III.	• Barbiturates • Narcotics • Stimulants
SCHEDULE V A low potential for abuse relative to the substances listed in Schedule III; currently accepted medical use in the United States; limited physical or psychological dependence relative to the substances listed in Schedule IV.	• Compounds with limited codeine such as cough medicine

Facts About Hallucinogens

LSD

Lysergic acid diethylamide-25, the full chemical name for LSD, is a synthesized derivative of an ergot—a toxic mold—that grows on rye.

LSD is also referred to as acid, windowpane, and sunshine.

LSD is commonly distributed on impregnated paper or stamps (blotter acid), in tablets (microdots), on thin squares of gelatin (windowpane), and on sugar cubes. Rarely, it is available in liquid form.

The average effective dose of LSD is twenty to eighty micrograms, with larger doses lasting ten to twelve hours.

The immediate physical effects of ingesting LSD may include dilated pupils, lowered body temperature, nausea, sweating, and increased heart rate.

After the first hour after ingesting LSD, users encounter mood changes; impaired judgment; racing and/or fragmented thoughts; distorted perceptions of objects, movements, colors, sound, and touch; and an altered sense of time and depth. Users often report synesthesia—"hearing colors" and "seeing sounds." These experiences may be pleasurable or extremely frightening.

The aftereffects of LSD may include anxiety and depression. Flashbacks—reexperiencing the effects of LSD use—may also occur days or months afterward, especially during times of stress.

LSD can cause psychotic episodes in some individuals, particularly in the mentally ill and those with untreated and/or unrecognized mental disorders.

More than 12 percent of high school seniors and college students have taken LSD at least once.

PCP

PCP, or phencyclidine, was initially created as a veterinary anesthetic in 1959.

Phencyclidine is also referred to as angel dust, embalming fluid, rocket fuel, wack, and ozone.

PCP is sold as a white, tan, or brown powder that can be dissolved in water. It may also be sold in tablet or capsule form. It most commonly appears as a powder or liquid that is applied to oregano, parsley, mint, or marijuana, and smoked.

The effects of PCP usage often include numbness, slurred speech, involuntary eye movements, loss of coordination, and visual and auditory distortions.

Some users of PCP experience anxiety, paranoia, violent hostility, psychotic breaks, and amnesia.

Psilocybin

Psilocybin, part of a class of chemicals known as tryptamines, is the psychoactive element found in *Psilocybe mexicana*, mushrooms that are native to tropical and subtropical regions of South America, Mexico, and the United States.

Psilocybin is commonly known as mushrooms, magic mushrooms, or "shrooms."

Psilocybin can also be synthesized and made available in tablets. Doses of ten to twenty milligrams create hallucinogenic effects.

Eating dried or brewed psilocybin mushrooms generally causes nausea, dilated pupils, and muscle relaxation. Its hallucinogenic effects are less predictable than those resulting from taking synthetic psilocybin, but may include mild to moderate visual and auditory distortions, euphoria, and changes in emotion and mood.

Peyote

Peyote refers to various species of psychoactive cacti, including *Lophophora williamsii* and *Lophophora lewinii*.

Peyote is ingested by eating the disk-shaped "buttons" that are visible on the crowns of peyote cactus plants. The buttons may be chewed or soaked in water to produce an intoxicating liquid.

Mescaline (3,4,5 trimethoxyphenethylamine) is a psychoactive element in peyote, which may be extracted from peyote or produced synthetically. Hallucinogenic doses are 0.3 to 0.5 grams and last for up to twelve hours.

Eating peyote buttons often results in nausea and vomiting.

An hour after taking peyote, users may experience euphoria; intensified visual impressions; an altered sense of time, space, and body awareness; mood swings; and feelings of self-transcendence.

Peyote use is illegal in the United States except for members of the Native American Church, who ingest the cactus as a ceremonial and spiritual practice.

Jimsonweed

Jimsonweed, or *Datura stamonium*, is a plant with leafy stems, white flowers, and prickly seed pods. It grows up to five feet in height.

Datura is also referred to as thornapple, locoweed, Jamestown weed, or fireweed.

Users gather and smoke datura leaves when the plant is in flower between May and September.

Smoking jimsonweed results in dilated pupils; slurred speech; confusion; rapid heartbeat; dry, flushed skin; impaired coordination; visual and auditory delusions; and delirium.

Jimsonweed is not listed in the Controlled Substances Act in the United States, but is considered one of the most dangerous hallucinogens. It can cause intense sensory distortions, seizures, cardiac arrest, and death.

1882

Harvard University psychologist William James publishes a paper about the subjective metaphysical effects of nitrous oxide.

1887

J.R. Briggs, a physician from Texas, writes an article describing his experience taking peyote, a hallucinogenic cactus that had been used for thousands of years in the religious rituals of Native Americans of Mexico.

1888

German researcher Louis Lewin publishes the first scientific report on the effect of peyote extract on animals.

1895

Mescaline is isolated as one of the psychoactive elements in the peyote cactus.

1897

British physician Havelock Ellis publishes a personal account of peyote intoxication in a medical journal.

1912

MDMA, a hallucinogen later known as Ecstasy, is synthesized by the Merck pharmaceutical company.

1919

Mescaline is first synthesized from the peyote cactus.

1938

Swiss chemist Albert Hofmann first synthesizes LSD-25 at the Sandoz drug company in Basel, Switzerland. The drug is tested on animals, but pharmacologists do not find the results interesting enough to pursue further research on it. The federal Food, Drug, and Cosmetic Act requires peyote to be sold with a label stating that it may be habit-forming.

1943

While researching potential circulatory stimulants, Hofmann again synthesizes LSD-25 and has a mild hallucinogenic experience after accidentally absorbing some of the drug through the skin of his fingers. Three days later, he self-administers a higher dose of the drug, inducing terrifying hallucinations. Hofmann concludes that the new drug may be useful in psychological research.

1949
LSD is introduced to the United States at the Boston Psychopathic Hospital, where research on its psychoactive properties begins.

1951
The U.S. Central Intelligence Agency (CIA) begins conducting research on LSD for potential weapons and espionage purposes.

1953
The first clinic using LSD for psychotherapy is established at Powick Hospital in England. Several U.S. donors, universities, and foundations, including the National Institute for Mental Health (NIMH), begin funding LSD research.

1954
Aldous Huxley publishes *The Doors of Perception*, an account of his experience taking mescaline under the supervision of British psychiatrist Humphry Osmond. Psychiatrist Oscar Janiger conducts private research on LSD. His volunteer subjects include actors Cary Grant and Jack Nicholson.

1955
A meeting of the American Psychiatric Association in Atlantic City, New Jersey, includes a symposium on hallucinogenic drugs.

1956
Beatnik writers Allen Ginsberg and William Burroughs write about their experiences with *yage*, a psychoactive tea from the Amazon.

1958
Hofmann isolates and synthesizes psilocybin from hallucinogenic mushroom *psilocybe mexicana*.

1959
Hofmann isolates lysergic acid amides from morning glory (*ololiuqui*) seeds. Phencyclidine (PCP) is introduced. Novelist Ken Kesey takes LSD, peyote, PCP, and other drugs as an experimental volunteer at a veteran's hospital in Menlo Park, California.

1960
Psychology instructors Timothy Leary and Richard Alpert, along with graduate students in Harvard's Center for Research in Personality, begin a series of experiments with hallucinogens.

1961
Leary begins his self-experiments with LSD. He and his colleagues also administer psilocybin to inmates in Concord Prison with the hopes of reducing recidivism.

1962
Doctoral candidate Walter Pahnke, along with his academic adviser Leary, conducts the "Good Friday" experiment in which several seminary students are given psilocybin to see if the drug induces mystical experiences.

1963
An amendment to the 1938 Food, Drug, and Cosmetic Act requires FDA approval for research involving humans and experimental drugs. Hereafter, psychedelic drugs are supplied only to government-funded researchers. Harvard University fires Leary and Alpert after reports that they gave hallucinogens to undergraduate students.

1964
Ken Kesey and the Merry Pranksters travel across the country in a refurbished school bus, taking hallucinogens and hosting "acid tests."

1965
A new law criminalizes the manufacturing and selling of hallucinogens, with the exception of distributors who sell to approved medical researchers. The majority of LSD researchers are required to stop their studies and return their drug supplies.

1966
The Merry Pranksters stage the three-day "Trips Festival," a concert and psychedelic exhibition, in San Francisco, California. Organizers provide attendees with LSD.

1967
In January, twenty-five thousand gather in San Francisco's Golden Gate Park for the first Human Be-In, a countercultural music and arts festival designed to unite political activists and the psychedelic movement. Thousands of hippies congregate in the city's Haight-Ashbury district for the LSD-inspired "Summer of Love." Researcher

Maimon Cohen publishes an article in *Science* claiming that LSD causes chromosome damage. The National Institute of Mental Health halts its research on hallucinogens.

1968
The Bureau of Narcotics and Dangerous Drugs, under the authority of the Department of Justice, is formed. The bureau is charged with prosecuting the nonmedical use of hallucinogens. In October, LSD possession becomes illegal.

1969
The three-day Woodstock rock festival takes place in upstate New York in August. LSD circulates among the more than 450,000 people in the audience. In December, cult leader Charles Manson, who had used LSD to brainwash his followers, is arrested for instigating several grisly murders in the Los Angeles area. Contaminated LSD is given out at the Altamont rock festival in Livermore, California, contributing to an atmosphere of violence at the concert that culminates in four deaths.

1970
The Controlled Substances Act establishes a set of five schedules for classifying drugs, with different degrees of control for each level. Most hallucinogens are placed in Schedule I, a classification for drugs that have no medical value but a high potential for abuse. Leary is imprisoned on drug charges, but he escapes and goes into exile.

1971
Researcher Norman I. Dishotsky announces that there is no evidence that LSD causes chromosome damage or birth defects.

1973
Leary is found in Afghanistan and returned to prison in the United States.

1976
Leary is released from prison. Chemist Alexander Shulgin creates a new synthesizing process for MDMA. Some psychotherapists quietly begin using MDMA in their clinical practices.

1988
MDMA, now commonly known as Ecstasy, is designated a Schedule I drug.

1989

The Food and Drug Administration (FDA) establishes Pilot Drug, a new review board. The board approves of research on medical marijuana and psychedelic drugs, ushering in a new era of scientific inquiry on hallucinogens.

1994

Ritual use of peyote among members of the Native American Church is declared legal.

1995

The Pilot Drug evaluation board is dissolved.

1996

Leary dies.

The editors have compiled the following list of organizations concerned with the issues debated in this book. The descriptions are derived from materials provided by the organizations. All have publications or information available for interested readers. The list was compiled on the date of publication of the present volume; the information provided here may change. Be aware that many organizations take several weeks or longer to respond to inquiries, so allow as much time as possible.

American Council for Drug Education (ACDE)
164 W. Seventy-fourth St., New York, NY 10023
(800) 488-3784 • (212) 595-5810, ext. 7860 • fax: (212) 595-2553
e-mail: acde@phoenixhouse.org • Web site: www.acde.org
The ACDE informs the public about the harmful effects of abusing drugs and alcohol. It gives the public access to scientifically based, compelling prevention programs and materials. ACDE has resources for parents, youths, educators, prevention professionals, employers, health care professionals, and other concerned community members who are working to help America's young people avoid the dangers of drug and alcohol abuse.

Canadian Foundation for Drug Policy (CFDP)
70 MacDonald St., Ottawa, ON K2P 1H6 Canada
(613) 236-1027 • fax: (613) 238-2891
e-mail: eoscapel@cfdp.ca • Web site: www.cfdp.ca
Founded by several of Canada's leading drug policy specialists, CFDP examines the objectives and consequences of Canada's drug laws and policies. When necessary, the foundation recommends alternatives that it believes would make Canada's drug policies more effective and humane. CFDP discusses drug policy issues with the Canadian government, media, and general public. It also disseminates educational materials and maintains a Web site with an archive of news articles, studies, and reports.

Drug Enforcement Administration (DEA)
Mailstop: AXS, 2401 Jefferson Davis Hwy., Alexandria, VA 22301
(202) 307-1000
Web site: www.usdoj.gov/dea
The DEA is the federal agency charged with enforcing the nation's drug laws. The agency concenrates on stopping the smuggling and the distribution of narcotics in the United States and abroad. It publishes the *Drug Enforcement Magazine* three times a year. The DEA Web site includes fact sheets on various hallucinogens and an explanation of the drug classification system.

Drug Policy Alliance
925 Fifteenth St. NW, Washington, DC 20005
(202) 216-0035 • fax: (202) 216-0803
e-mail: dc@drugpolicy.org • Web site: www.dpf.org

The Drug Policy Alliance is a merging of the Lindesmith Center, formerly the leading drug policy reform institute in the United States, and the Drug Policy Foundation, a nonprofit organization that advocated sensible and humane drug policies. These two organizations joined in the year 2000 with the objective of building a national drug policy reform movement. The alliance works to broaden the public debate on drug policy and to promote realistic alternatives to the war on drugs based on science, compassion, public health, and human rights. The Web site includes links to fact sheets, documents, and other Internet sources with information on hallucinogens and drug research.

Drug Reform Coordination Network
1623 Connecticut Ave. NW, Third Fl., Washington, DC 20009
(202) 293-8340 • fax: (202) 293-8344
e-mail: drcnet@drcnet.org • Web site: http://stopthedrugwar.org

Founded in 1993, the network has grown into a national and global organization including parents, educators, students, lawyers, health care professionals, and others working for drug policy reform from a variety of perspectives. The network promotes an open debate on drug prohibition and focuses on issues such as the reform of sentencing and forfeiture laws and the medicalization of current Schedule I drugs. The site features an extensive online library with links to research and articles about hallucinogens, including "Drugs and Mysticism" and "Therapeutic Applications of LSD and Related Drugs."

Multidisciplinary Association for Psychedelic Studies (MAPS)
2105 Robinson Ave., Sarasota, FL 34232
(941) 924-6277 • (888) 868-6277
e-mail: info@maps.org • Web site: www.maps.org

MAPS is a membership-based research and educational organization. It focuses on the development of beneficial, socially sanctioned uses of psychedelic drugs and marijuana. MAPS helps scientific researchers obtain government approval for, fund, conduct, and report on psychedelic research in human volunteers. It publishes the quarterly *MAPS Bulletin* as well as various reports and newsletters.

National Center on Addiction and Substance Abuse (CASA)
Columbia University
633 Third Ave., Nineteenth Fl., New York, NY 10017-6706
(212) 841-5200 • fax: (212) 956-8020
Web site: www.casacolumbia.org

CASA is a private nonprofit organization that works to educate the public about the hazards of chemical dependency. The organization supports treatment as the best way to reduce chemical dependency. It produces publications describing the harmful effects of alcohol and drug addiction and effective ways to address the problem of substance abuse.

National Clearinghouse for Alcohol and Drug Information
11426-28 Rockville Pike, Suite 200, Rockville, MD 20052
(800) 729-6686
e-mail: webmaster@health.org • Web site: www.health.org

The clearinghouse distributes publications of the U.S. Department of Health and Human Services, the National Institute on Drug Abuse, and other federal agencies concerned with alcohol and drug abuse. Papers available through its Web site include "Pulse Check: National Trends in Drug Abuse," and "Prevention Alert: Did 'Sixties Parents' Hurt Their Kids?"

National Institute on Drug Abuse (NIDA)
National Institutes of Health
6001 Executive Blvd., Room 5213, Bethesda, MD 20892-9561
(301) 443-1124
e-mail: information@lists.nida.nih.gov
Web site: www.nida.nih.gov

NIDA supports and conducts research on drug abuse—including the yearly Monitoring the Future Survey—to improve addiction prevention, treatment, and policy efforts. It publishes the bimonthly *NIDA Notes* newsletter, the periodic *NIDA Capsules* fact sheets, and a catalog of research reports and public education materials.

Office of National Drug Control Policy
Drug Policy Information Clearinghouse
PO Box 6000, Rockville, MD 20849-6000
e-mail: ondcp@ncjrs.org
Web site: www.whitehousedrugpolicy.gov

The Office of National Drug Control Policy is responsible for formulating the government's national drug strategy and the president's antidrug policy as well as coordinating the federal agencies responsible for stopping drug trafficking. Drug policy studies are available upon request.

Partnership for a Drug-Free America
405 Lexington Ave., Suite 1601, New York, NY 10174
(212) 922-1560 • fax: (212) 922-1570
Web site: www.drugfreeamerica.org

The Partnership for a Drug-Free America is a nonprofit organization that utilizes media communication to reduce demand for illicit drugs in America. Best known for its national antidrug advertising campaign, the partnership works to "unsell" drugs to children and to prevent drug abuse among youths. It publishes the annual *Partnership Newsletter* as well as monthly press releases about current events with which the partnership is involved.

Books

William Braden, *The Private Sea, LSD, and the Search for God.* Chicago: Quadrangle Books, 1967.

W.V. Caldwell, *LSD Psychotherapy: An Exploration of Psychedelic and Psycholytic Therapy.* New York: Grove Press, 1968.

Marilyn Carroll, *PCP: The Dangerous Angel.* New York: Chelsea House, 1992.

Sidney Cohen, *The Beyond Within: The LSD Story.* New York: Atheneum, 1966.

Marily Dobkin de Rios and Oscar Janiger, *LSD, Spirituality, and the Creative Process.* Rochester, VT: Park Street Press, 2003.

Paul Devereux, *The Long Trip: A Prehistory of Psychedelia.* New York: Penguin, 1997.

Peter T. Furst, *Mushrooms: Psychedelic Fungi.* New York: Chelsea House, 1992.

Stanislav Grof, *LSD Psychotherapy.* Alameda, CA: Hunter House, 1994.

Michael J. Harner, ed., *Hallucinogens and Shamanism.* New York: Oxford University Press, 1973.

Charles Hayes, ed., *Tripping: An Anthology of True-Life Psychedelic Adventures.* New York: Penguin, 1999.

Aldous Huxley, *The Doors of Perception.* New York: Harper & Row, 1963.

Mike Jay, ed., *Artificial Paradises: A Drugs Reader.* New York: Penguin, 1999.

Martin A. Lee and Bruce Schlain, *Acid Dreams: The Complete Social History of LSD: The CIA, the Sixties, and Beyond.* New York: Grove Weidenfeld, 1985.

Ralph Metzner, ed., *The Ecstatic Adventure.* New York: Macmillan, 1968.

Gerald Newman and Eleanor Newman Layfield, *PCP.* Springfield, NJ: Enslow, 1997.

Edward R. Ricciuti, *The Devil's Garden: Facts and Folklore of Perilous Plants.* New York: Walker, 1978.

Huston Smith, *Cleansing the Doors of Perception: The Religious Significance of Entheogenic Plants and Chemicals.* New York: Jeremy P. Tarcher/Putnam, 2000.

Nigel South, ed., *Drugs: Cultures, Controls, and Everyday Life.* Thousand Oaks, CA: Sage, 1999.

Jay Stevens, *Storming Heaven: LSD and the American Dream.* New York: Atlantic Monthly Press, 1987.

Michael E. Trulson, *LSD, Visions, or Nightmares.* New York: Chelsea House, 1985.

Periodicals

Stew Albert, "Death of a Salesman: Remembering Timothy Leary," *Tikkun*, September/October 1996.

Jeff Barker, "A 'Stigma' Erased: Bill Will Allow Native Americans to Use Peyote for Ceremonies," *Arizona Republic*, October 5, 1994.

Marco Barneveld, "Dope Trek: The Inside Story," *National Post*, March 25, 2000.

Tom Batchelder, "Drug Addictions, Hallucinogens, and Shamanism: The View from Anthropology," *Townsend Letter for Doctors and Patients*, July 2001.

Bret Blosser, "The Return of the Peyoteros," *Whole Earth Review*, Summer 1992.

Robert Faggen and Ken Kesey, "The Great American Hollow," *Harper's Magazine*, August 1994.

Martin Gardner, "Carlos Castaneda and New Age Anthropology," *Skeptical Inquirer*, September/October 1999.

Adele Getty, "Twists of Fate," *ReVision*, Winter 2003.

Lester Grinspoon and Rick Doblin, "Psychedelics as Catalysts of Insight-Oriented Psychotherapy," *Social Research*, Fall 2001.

Peter Hadfield, "Freaky Fungi in Japan," *U.S. News & World Report*, August 6, 2001.

Charles Hayes, "Is Taking a Psychedelic an Act of Sedition?" *Tikkun*, March 2002.

Barry L. Jacobs, "How Hallucinogenic Drugs Work," *American Scientist*, July/August 1987.

Kathiann M. Kowalski, "What Hallucinogens Can Do to Your Brain," *Current Health 2*, April 2000.

Paul Lashmar, "Come Fly with Me," *New Statesman & Society*, June 25, 1993.

Robert Leiby, "The Magical Mystery Cure," *Esquire*, September 1997.

Dana Mackenzie, "Secrets of an Acid Head," *New Scientist*, June 23, 2001.

Andrew Maykuth, "An African Shrub That Got Him off Heroin and Cocaine," *Philadelphia Inquirer*, July 4, 1992.

Kelly Morris, "High Time We Cleaned Up on Drugs," *Lancet*, February 10, 2001.

John B. Murray, "Phencyclidine (PCP): A Dangerous Drug, but Useful in Schizophrenia Research," *Journal of Psychology*, May 2002.

Newsweek, "Turned-On Way of Life," November 28, 1966.

David Porush, "Finding God," *Omni*, October 1993.

Kira Salak, "Lost Souls of the Peyote Trail," *National Geographic Adventure*, August 2002.

Joshua Wolf Shenk, "Why You Can Hate Drugs and Still Want to Legalize Them," *Washington Monthly*, October 1995.

Alexander T. Shulgin, "Confessions of a Psychedelic Alchemist," *Whole Earth Review*, Fall 1991.

Suzanne Smalley and Debra Rosenberg, "'I Felt Like I Wanted to Hurt People': Emergency Rooms Report the Violent Return of PCP," *Newsweek*, July 22, 2002.

Colin Tudge, "A Drug-Free State Just Isn't Normal," *New Statesman*, January 9, 1998.

Andrew T. Weil, "The Strange Case of the Harvard Drug Scandal," *Look*, November 5, 1963.

INDEX